Entities Among Us

Also by Catherine Bowman
> *Crystal Awareness*
> *Crystal Ascension: Spiritual Growth & Planetary Healing*

Forthcoming
> *Conversation with Soul: Lifting the Veil*
> *Daughter of the Flame*

"Catherine Bowman has truly original insight into unseen energies that affect all of us. She combines extensive personal experience with practical solutions to rid the menacing vibrations in our lives. You will discover what energies rob you of vitality, haunt your home, lower productivity in your office, induce fear, cause depression, and trigger illness. By following Ms. Bowman's practical step-by-step straightforward instructions to clear these unwanted sources, you will be able to reach into the higher realms of awareness."
> —Dr. Frank Alper, Adamis Enterprises, Switzerland

"Catherine Bowman's *Entities Among Us* is a knowledgeable, insightful guide filled with wonderful practical ideas on how to deal with unwanted energies. It expands our perception on how unseen energies flow through and around us. Bowman's book is an important addition to anyone exploring life beyond the five senses."
> —Carolyn Kaganovsky N.D.

"The theme of *Entities Among Us* is that there are unseen forces that are present in all of our lives that affect our well being. Ms. Bowman gently awakens her readers to sense the world beyond the obvious. She gives us much to think about with her insightful views on certain people draining our energies, the presence of ghosts causing havoc in our lives, the after-effects of out-of-body and near-death experiences, karmic attachments and the lingering effects from negative places. She has written a readable, thought-provoking work on how our awareness needs to change in order for us to fully live and work in the light."
> —Nadia Haridi M.B.A Cairo, Egypt

ENTITIES AMONG US

*Unseen Forces That
Affect Our Daily Lives*

CATHERINE BOWMAN

Blue Dolphin Publishing

Published by Blue Dolphin Publishing, Inc.
P.O. Box 8, Nevada City, CA 95959
Orders: 1-800-643-0765
www.bluedolphinpublishing.com

ISBN: 1-57733-083-8

Library of Congress Cataloging-in-Publication Data

Bowman, Catherine, 1953-
    Entities among us : unseen forces that affect our daily lives/
Catherine Bowman.
        p. cm.
Includes bibliographical references.
    ISBN 1-57733-083-8
    1. Demonology. 2. Ghosts. 3. Exorcism. I. Title.

    BL480B69 2003
    133.9—dc21

                                              2001042975

Cover design: Jeff Case

First Printing: May, 2003

Printed in the United States of America

5   4   3   2   1

This is my truth
Mississauga, Ontario

Dedicated in love and light
To my parents Effie and Marven,
My husband, Ralph,
And my son, Adam.

Without their understanding and loving support,
the writing of this book would not be possible.

A special thank you to my father, who devoted many hours
to editing this manuscript.

And special thanks to those people and spirits who
helped make this book a reality.

Contents

KNOW THYSELF

Delphi Oracle

Preface

DURING BOOK SIGNINGS AND CRYSTAL SEMINARS on my first two books, *Crystal Awareness* (1987) and *Crystal Ascension* (1997), many readers, earnestly seeking a deeper understanding of self, expressed concerns as to why negative forces were affecting their lives. Always intrigued by the contradiction of working in the light while being challenged by lower, darker forces, my challenge became how to explain this anomaly to readers without deterring or discouraging them from pursuing their spiritual growth.

When I began researching and writing this book, I had many challenges from unseen forces endeavoring to prevent its completion and publication. My work was constantly being interrupted by diversions, sent to test my inner convictions about the unseen vibrations that are around each and every one of us. It was not uncommon to experience power outages, which meant the loss of several manuscript pages and precious time on the computer. Many unforeseen family crises and health issues diverted my attention. Taped interviews with colleagues either "mysteriously" missed being recorded or the sound was so distorted that the information was unintelligible. Books would disappear that I needed for research, and my house was invaded by creatures not of this world.

The motivation to overcome these and other obstacles was fortified by the desire to help others avoid the pitfalls that can occur when opening up to spiritual forces without proper protection. Many years ago I made the conscious choice to commit to my spiritual journey. Since then, experiences with entity possessions, ghosts, poltergeists, negative thought forms, psychic attacks and human parasites have convinced me the time has come to inform others of the energies that test our resolve and faith.

With high levels of energy that are currently being channeled onto our planet, as Beings of Light it is our right to know **if we are under attack, what the source of that negative energy is, how to combat it,** and most importantly, **what precautions are needed to protect ourselves.**

Acknowledgments

T HE FOLLOWING PEOPLE contributed their knowledge and/or help in the writing of *Entities Among Us*. I thank each and every one of them.

Frank Alper
Helene Laura Ampell
Nino Balbaa
Tim Balbaa
Raouf Balbaa
Effie Bowman
Marven Bowman
Kevin Fitzpatrick
Jeanie Harmer
Carolyn Kaganowsky
Adrian Kronberg
Jody Maas
Lois and Harvey Macklin
Mary Jean Muir
Greg Nolan
Carolyn Ostrowski
Bart Smit

INTRODUCTION

The Next Stage of Awareness

A NEW STAGE OF SPIRITUAL GROWTH HAS ARRIVED with a greater number of people choosing to willfully alter their consciousness. Prior to the dawn of the millennium, only limited numbers were seeking higher wisdom. In the twentieth century, names such as Allister Crowley, Madame Blavatsky, Alice Bailey, Vera Adler, Dion Fortune and Edgar Cayce made headlines for their mystical revelations. In the psychedelic era of the sixties, flower children sparked an interest in ancient philosophies and Eastern religious practices. During the 80s and early 90s, crystals, channelling, meditation, alternative healing, flower and gem remedies were in vogue. Then, in the late nineties, a new wave of spirituality permeated society. More and more people were opening to higher consciousness.

The millennium has projected all of us into an accelerated state of soul evolution. A NEW CENTURY is unfolding, bringing into conscious expression powerful healing energies, synchronicity with others, creativity, intuition, prosperity and a host of other higher attributes.

Many of us are undergoing spontaneous spiritual awakenings. A sudden urge prompts us to read a certain thought-

1

provoking book or attend a self-help seminar. Some may be drawn to work with the energies of crystals or gemstones. Others may decide to consult a psychic or channeler. A chance encounter with a certain someone may be the turning point, triggering the interest to pursue an inner journey. Whatever the source of awakening, a doorway is opened to another realm of consciousness. CONSCIOUS EFFORT IS APPLIED TO SERIOUSLY EXAMINE INNER BELIEFS AND IMPLEMENT CHANGE.

Alternatively, a forced spiritual awakening can also be invoked by a near-death experience (N.D.E.), the death of a loved one, divorce, a life-threatening disease or some other crisis, any of which can result in a surge of desire to begin the process of spiritual apprenticeship. It is during this time that a period of adjustment, whether from a gentle awakening or a life-altering traumatic experience, can result in our having difficulty coping with the ups and downs of daily living. There is conflict with previous beliefs and attitudes. However, as we undergo the transformation from **self** to **higher self**, we still need to function in this world. While this metamorphosis is occurring, few of us enjoy the luxury of total isolation from the responsibilities of day-to-day living. Instead, we are busy working at jobs, being parents, spouses, family members, partners, friends, community workers and so forth.

We live in a world where many of our experiences cannot be seen with the physical eyes. Most of the time the veil of the third dimension shrouds us from an awareness of "seeing" and "sensing" other aspects of our lives. It is only when this curtain is lifted through meditation, using crystals, balancing our chakras, a healing treatment or life-altering event that we sense and experience beyond our current scope or capacity. Intuition is acutely heightened. There is a flickering of déjà vu. We intuit what the other person is about to say. The caller on the phone is identified before the receiver is lifted. We know that job offer is coming or that someone is about to visit. We sense when a loved one has died. All of these examples are outside the laws of our physical world. It is only when we step beyond and acknowledge the unseen facets of our lives that we become free of restricted thinking. Then we can perceive the wonderment and knowingness of dimensions beyond this realm. Yet, even though a conscious decision has been made to connect with our inner self and higher consciousness, many of us are held back from fully moving into these wondrous states by detrimental energies that have inadvertently been attracted to our auras.

We are probably going to be, have been or presently are the victim of some form of energy invasion. The closer we move into the light, the more sensitive we become to unseen forces of both a positive and negative nature.

The following list will help you to ascertain whether one or several of these occurrences **has** or **is** happening;

- **Unseen forces are sensed around you.**
- **You are overwhelmed by thoughts totally foreign to your character, i.e., thoughts of revenge, road rage, quitting your job, leaving your family**
- **Suicidal thoughts enter your mind**
- **You have mood swings for no apparent reason**
- **You are drained to the point of exhaustion after being in the company of certain people**
- **You have a sense of foreboding upon entering certain buildings or houses**
- **Your skin feels clammy and goose bumps appear while in certain places**
- **A crushing heaviness on your chest jars you awake at night**
- **Annoying, trivial dreams of events, people and conversations that occurred during the day, rob you of deep sleep**
- **You smell foul odors and cannot trace the source**

- Objects disappear only to reappear later
- In certain rooms there are unexplainable changes in air temperature
- You cross your wrists or place your hands over your solar plexus when conversing with some people

If you or someone you know has experienced or is experiencing one or more of the above conditions, **foreign energies are attacking.**

The next stage of spiritual awareness has arrived; *ENTITIES ARE AMONG US.*

*And many of those who sleep in the dust of the earth shall awake,
some to everlasting life, and some to shame
and everlasting contempt.*

Daniel 12:2

CHAPTER ONE

Death:
The Transition

DEATH IS PART OF LIFE, affecting each of us in different ways. It is impossible to pass through life without experiencing the trauma of losing a loved one. We are born into a physical body that is left behind at death. Because we cannot fully experience death while living, it is only natural that religions and cultures have varying ideas of what transpires when the soul leaves the body. Christians believe in heaven, where angels are waiting to guide the righteous through the pearly gates, where there is no pain and eternal life is guaranteed. Hell is a place of fire and damnation, an assured destination if the ten commandments are ignored. Others embrace the idea of purgatory, where the soul is held while being judged.

To Buddhists and Hindus, death is a release of the soul, depending on the behavior of the person while on earth, into paradise, Nirvana, or hell.

In Islam, the dead are sent to Paradise if they have been good Muslims, while infidels are banished to hell.

The Jewish faith teaches resurrection and subsequent judgment of the dead.

The hunting tribes of the North American Indians believe the Happy Hunting Ground is the place to which one went after death, full of the bounties of the earth.

Those who perceive it as finality, fear death. It is the end of all. A 1990 Gallup Poll survey (USA) states that 71% of the population believe in life after death while 19% do not, and the rest have no opinion. In the past few years, there have been many books and articles written about near-death experiences (N.D.E.), all affirming life after death. The commonality in all these accounts is a release from pain, the sensation of floating above the physical body, seeking out family members and being drawn towards a bright light. The general population further seems to be more open to the possibility of life beyond death by the popularity of movies such as *Ghost, Like Water for Chocolate, City of Angels, The House of Spirits* and *Michael*, all portraying a life beyond this plane.

Channelers and psychics receive messages from discarnate beings. Persons who have past-life regressions are assured of the soul's immortality. Like the Death Card in the Tarot deck, death is merely a transition, a completion of one cycle and the beginning of a new one. Slowly the skeptical populace is being convinced that there is perhaps more to death and spirits than meets the eye.

Life after death is eternal and timeless. Every civilization has a religious dogma that makes sense and order of the afterlife. Early records portray ancient Egyptians making exhaustive preparations for the safe voyage of corpses into the afterlife. It was of outmost importance that the personality (kA) and soul (BA) safely reach into the next world so the spirit wouldn't be earthbound. This elaborate preparation of the dead had great significance as it is written in the Egyptian Book of the Dead. Hieroglyphics depict Osiris (light) being dismembered by his brother Set (dark). Osiris brought peace and the reason for existence to Egyptians by establishing laws and rituals for worshipping Gods. Set, extremely jealous of his brother's popularity, tricked him into lying in a wooden box. This live prison was then set afloat on the Nile and washed out to sea. From there it landed on a distant shore and was caught in the center of a growing tamarisk tree. A king had the tree cut down (unaware of the box) and made it into a supporting pillar for his palace. When Isis, Osiris's wife, discovered what had happened to her beloved, she had the pillar cut open and the box removed. But once again, Set apprehended his brother, this time cutting him into fourteen pieces which were scattered over Egypt, which Isis later collected. The legend is that Osiris then became the God of Eternal Life.

The intricate funeral arrangements of removing the dead person's vital organs and embalming the body originate from this story. Tombs of nobleman and pharaohs in the Valley of the Kings are filled with special household articles such as chairs, beds and pottery to comfort their BA in the afterlife. Hieroglyphics, painted on tomb walls, ensured a smooth transition and burial sites were protected by curses to deter robbers from disturbing the remains. The dead needed an undisturbed transition to ensure their souls would not be trapped in the astral plane.

The Egyptians were not the only culture to believe in life after death; ancient Greeks and Romans had an afterworld. In the *Odyssey*, Homer tells of a place where it was eternally spring, Elysium, while Hades ruled the underworld. Both Homer and Aeneas descended into the bowels of the earth where deceased family members met them.

The philosopher, Socrates, received his prophetic teachings from an unearthly guide. It was this discarnate that urged him to his death. Plato wrote about the immortality of the soul. Greeks believed in communication with spirits and

Gods as evidenced by the Delphi oracles. The Bible's New Testament alludes to an existence beyond the earth plane. Jesus revived others from the dead and he himself arose.

The Middle Ages recognized and believed that certain people received extraordinary powers from unearthly beings. Joan of Arc was burned in 1431 for hearing spirit voices and heeding their advice. In that era countless individuals, especially women, were accused of conferring with Satan and evil spirits. In the book *We Don't Die,* George Anderson wrote that over 200,000 people were tortured and burned at the stake for witchcraft. The repercussion of this mass hysteria has flowed over into modern life. Some of us still are afraid to stand up for our beliefs for fear of persecution. Many new-agers, through past-life regressions, have discovered they were in fact accused of witchcraft in previous lives.

I was plagued by such a haunting memory until I was able to release its hold and begin writing my books. I was persecuted, in my incarnation during the 1500s, for my work with dream interpretation, crystals, discarnates and herbal remedies. Through regression, I relived my imprisonment, torture and subsequent burning. I could see my tattered clothes, the jeering crowds, feel the heat of the fire and smell the stench of burning flesh. I also saw the person who had accused me of witchcraft. In this present life, this person's karma was overcome by helping me find my latent psychic abilities and pushing me to once again embrace my spirituality.

Death is not final. The physical body reverts to dust but consciousness goes on, and it is the level of this consciousness that dictates where the soul will go in the spiritual realm. Some do not even realize their physical self has died, continuing on just as if they were alive. And it is these lost souls that cause some interesting complications in our lives.

CHAPTER TWO

Spirit Hierarchy – Up the Ladder

BEFORE ADDRESSING THE DIFFERENT TYPES of entities and how these spirits are attracted to us, an understanding of the various dimensions that exist beyond our reality must be established.

We should not think of the physical and spiritual world as separate, unrelated planes. Not only is each as real as the other but one affects the other. As above, so below.

THE LEVELS

Our planet has a number of energy levels radiating beyond it. Depending on which authorities are consulted, there can be from three to twelve different dimensions. Since there is no one, authentic authority, for the purposes of this book, the six levels considered are the astral, causal, angelic, master, archangel and Creator planes. The diagram, Spiritual Hierarchy, depicts these layers.

Each plane or level affects the one beneath it, in turn controlled by the one above it. Because we tend to think in linear terms, it is easier for the purpose of this discussion to imagine these planes piled one on top of the other. They are however, in reality, interrelated. It may be easier to think of them as radio bands we can tune into. By simply adjusting our consciousness, we can attune to the astral, causal or the higher levels.

THIRD DIMENSION AND SOUL

The third dimension is the area with which we are obviously most familiar and comfortable. It consists of solids, liquids and gases, and has a dense vibratory rate. We know these elements exist as they are readily discerned by our five senses.

SPIRITUAL HIERARCHY

CREATOR

ARCHANGELS

MASTERS

ANGELS

CAUSAL

ASTRAL

EARTH

UP THE LADDER

The third dimension is the school for our souls' growth and development where very rapid soul evolution occurs. We are the soul's physical vehicle for accomplishing all it has been destined to achieve in a lifetime.

Every person has a soul. For eons it has alternated between the confinement of a body and the freedom of spirit. Yet, both are connected, for the body without a soul would be an empty shell.

The differences between body and soul are:

BODY	SOUL
Seen	Sensed
Dies	Eternal
Locked in 3rd dimension	Free to travel
Time oriented	Timeless
	(not restricted by time)
Waiting to die	Grows and evolves

The soul alerts its vehicle when something is amiss by giving the body health-related challenges/problems. If we are not speaking our truth or saying what we should, a sore throat may occur. With feelings of unworthiness, insecurity or fear of asserting our personal power, an ulcer or bowel trouble can develop. By being too giving towards others, sacrificing our needs, breast/chest problems have a possibility of arising. These are all messages from soul to consciousness saying, "SOMETHING IS NOT IN ORDER. YOU ARE NOT LISTENING TO ME!"

Whenever I contract an illness or injury, I always question what the lesson or learning experience means; what is soul trying to tell me? So, when I recently suffered a sprained ankle, I had some soul searching to do. My personality was refusing to comply with the direction life was currently moving me. I was not progressing with the completion of this manuscript. I felt there were very valid excuses as to why this was not the right time to do so. The injury was a gentle, yet subtle nudge to listen to my inner voice and start putting pen to paper.

Our souls are as much a part of the third dimension as our bodies. The seat of the soul is thought to be located over the heart chakra. When we are consciously connected with it, soul can be projected into our daily expression. In order to do this, we have to allow it access to our personality.

Personality tries to maintain a separate existence from soul, like teenagers rebelling against parental edicts. A young person believes that s/he is independent. Parental advice and guidance just isn't welcome until a situation occurs where s/he can't cope. The parent is then asked for help. Similarly, when we can no longer cope with the state of our lives and some incident such as an accident, death of a loved one, divorce, loss of a job or emotional shock upsets our belief system, the soul is called upon for help. It lingers, watching and waiting, while we suffer through life's trials and tribulations. Like a parent, it always shares our joys and sorrows and is ready to lend a helping hand. It quietly waits for us to turn within and ask for help and direction.

In this present age, many souls try the traditional route of organized religion, and if one finds these beliefs lacking, searches for meaning through metaphysical groups, books, seminars, healing and other paths to enlightenment. By being exposed to many different ways of thinking, teachings and beliefs, the soul then selects those most suitable for its evolvement.

To grow and evolve, conscious union with the soul must be achieved. Only then can we fulfill our reason for incarnating at this special time. The souls of the majority who have incarnated during this current age of Ascension have a mission to gain a deeper understanding of spirituality and raise the consciousness of humankind.

Unlimited light will manifest in our lives when soul is given freedom to guide and direct us to overcome life's daily strife and discord. Each of our souls has made the commitment to fully express themselves, thereby nudging the conscious personality to slowly retire into the background, as it merges with soul. **We then become a beautiful duality of light, a burning flame of love.**

THE ASTRAL PLANE

The next level is the astral or fourth dimension, less dense than the third, vibrating at a faster rate. Objects reflect light rather than being in solid form. This is the plane to which we travel during sleep. Here, we instantaneously think of being somewhere and we are there. We effortlessly walk through walls and on top of water. There are no third-dimensional barriers.

Unlike earth, where time is a huge factor, everything happens instantaneously through the will of the spirits. They can dematerialize or materialize at will in various shapes and forms. This is why we often see our deceased relatives and loved ones in happy, healthy, youthful forms.

Several years ago, while living in Toronto, I sensed the transition of my Aunt Jean who was being hospitalized in Montreal. My meditation was interrupted by a vision of my aunt at her favorite lakeside retreat. She appeared young, full of vitality and extremely happy. In reality she was in her late eighties, wasting away with cancer. I did not learn, until later, that she died at the same time I had seen her. This image, of her in perfect health and harmony, helped me to not overly grieve her passing. I was pleased that she was finally free of pain and enjoying herself.

The astral has many layers of energy and soul levels. First, and closest to earth, are those beings who have just passed away through natural, suicidal or accidental death. A goodly number are temporarily, lost souls. They cannot accept or understand why they no longer have a physical body. Depending on their spiritual development, the number of lifetimes on earth and lessons completed, they may either progress to higher levels or stay in this dimension. Those who remain are earth bound due to the excessive grieving of loved ones, the need to seek revenge, addictions, having committed suicide, or being too spiritually naive to move toward the light.

These misguided, trapped souls have the potential of manifesting as ghosts, poltergeists, monsters and other unsavory characters. They can haunt people, places and invade our energy fields; they are lost souls, seeking help.

If we were able to consciously tour the astral plane, we would see many differences from the physical. In *The Autobiography of a Yogi*, a teacher describes this plane as "infinitely beautiful, clean, pure and orderly. The terrestrial blemishes—weeds, bacteria, insects, snakes—are absent." The author goes on to say the temperature is perfect, like an eternal spring. He relates that there are two kinds of spirits in the astral, those waiting to return to earth and those waiting to go on to the higher planes.

THE CAUSAL PLANE

Above the astral is the causal or mental plane. Vibrations here are even higher, oscillating at more accelerated frequencies. The inhabitants of this level lend nonjudgmental aid to people and all living matter on earth. These spirits are our teachers and guides, being more spiritually evolved than the souls of the astral plane. They have opted to work with us, while at the same time working on their own spiritual evolution, for they too must climb the ladder of spiritual hierarchy. The ultimate goal of each soul, no matter which plane it is on, is to return to the Creator level. So all the while these entities are with us, they are receiving higher teachings from the upper dimensions.

Throughout our lifetime, different guides and teachers will manifest, work with us, and then leave when their task is completed. Guides, having an expertise in one particular area, are here to assist us in that specific field. For instance, if you were working on a particular project, involved in a task that requires concentration and effort for a period of time, these spirits would be available to work with you. And as your projects and goals change, so do guides.

As a young girl, I was aware of an Indian spirit guide who would help me with my studying. I sensed this being directing me to the subjects I needed to learn. Later, when I was working on my crystal books, I called on and received help from different spirit guides who were experts in crystal healing. Even while writing this passage, I felt ever-patient presences helping me understand spirit hierarchy.

Teachers/masters work to bring us closer to our souls and spirituality. A teacher is not allowed to live a human's life, just assist. They direct us to certain people, books, places and circumstances to enhance spiritual progress.

Just as we advanced through the educational system, switching teachers with each higher grade, we also change our spiritual teachers as our level of awareness evolves. Such entities can be contacted and communicated with through meditation, prayer, or by simply being receptive to their higher council. When I first started to consciously work with my etheric teachers and guides, I doubted my contact. I thought it was imagination. I would "feel" the presence of higher energies as my consciousness progressed and at rare times saw their images surrounded by a luminous white light. There is no mistaking that they are entities of higher levels as my physical body tingled and resonated in harmony.

Masters often materialize in our minds or, in some cases their presence is sensed around our bodies when we are at our lowest moment. They lift us spiritually, renewing our hope and faith.

Whenever I can't cope with any more discord from work or my family, I meditate and ask that light and love be poured into my being. I am never refused or disappointed. I feel the healing rays soothing, calming and removing the negativity from my emotional and mental fields.

CLIMBING TO THE HIGHEST LEVELS – ANGELIC, ARCHANGEL AND CREATOR LEVELS

Inspiration, wisdom, guidance, creativity, universal truths, healing techniques and understanding are available from the higher levels. This Universal Consciousness descends or filters through the various levels to permeate all the levels below. Some of these rays reach earth and are absorbed by our auric field.

The levels above the fifth differ according to various teachings. For the purpose of comprehending the hierarchy of entities, the next dimension is the Angelic Level. The vibrations here are concerned with even higher vibrations than the causal plane. This is the level where the realms of angels reside. These Beings are capable of coming down to earth level when their services are needed. Most people refer to Beings from this level as guardian angels, the servants of the Creator. They watch over us. And watching over the angels are the Archangels, the Creator's helpers.

Dionysious the Aeropagite, in sixth-century Greece, depicted nine orders of angels in his book, *The Celestial Hierar-*

chy. He further subdivided the nine, with the highest being the closest to God. He called them Seraphim, Cherubim, Thrones, Dominions, Virtues, Powers, Principalities, Archangels and Angels. Dionysious gave them specific assignments (see Harvey Humann, *The Many Faces of Angels*).

There are numerous Biblical references to these celestial beings. "See, I am sending an angel before you to guard you on the way and bring you to a place I have prepared..." (Exod. 23:20) was one of the many divine laws decreed to mankind. "And I saw an angel come down from heaven, having the key of the bottomless pit and a chain in his hand" (Rev. 20:1) refers to the first resurrection. In Daniel 10, the archangel Michael was referred to as a great Prince who stood for all of mankind.

In the 1990s, there was a big revival of interchanges with Angels. Individuals told more of their personal experiences with these Beings. Lightworkers believed frequent visitations and visions were signs of hope and enlightenment for this planet. We can now consciously seek all levels of the angelic realm for their heavenly assistance to bring joy, harmony and peace into our lives.

These spirits are here to serve humankind and all souls. Everyone appears to have at least one guardian angel. We often say, "An angel must be looking after me," after being saved from some sort of close call. Although we don't see our guardian angel, we sense its protectiveness.

Angels can assume three-dimensional form to get our attention. Gabriel appeared to Zacharis telling him of the coming of John. This same being spoke to Mary, announcing she was to give birth to Christ. Gabriel materialized to Mohammed and recited the Holy Book, the Koran. Angels came to warn Abraham before the destruction of Sodom and Gomorrah.

These groups of spirits are duty-bound to serve mankind and all souls. They teach souls on the casual plane who in turn guide the astral souls and are available for us to call on for assistance. Some well-known archangels are Michael, Gabriel, Raphael and Metatron. Michael is the Creator's angel leading the battle of light over darkness. He threw Satan out of Heaven. Michael is also the angel of the Last Judgment, who weighs our souls at transition. Raphael is the Angel of Healing and nurturing. He is very attuned to those on their spiritual path. Metatron watches over the children of Israel. In the Book of Genesis, Metatron was originally a normal man, Enoch, before becoming a scribe for God. Archangels protect us from harmful energies and comfort us in times of spiritual confusion. At this time there is more contact with these heavenly beings than ever because of the devastating conditions of our world.

The last rung of the ladder is the Creator, the Source of all thoughts, energy and soul creation. This Supreme Being watches over the spiritual and third-dimensional worlds.

SPIRIT COMMUNICATION

Spirits communicate with us in a hierarchical order. Lesser souls cannot travel up in this pyramidal organization; they are trapped in the lower zones and can't travel upwards. If a young soul were to pass over that had committed mass murder, he would be confined to the lower part of the astral level for further soul evolvement and teachings. If this person's mother were on the fifth level, he could not contact her. He would be forced to wait for her soul to come down to him.

When a higher dimensional spirit wishes to contact a lower entity, it can send a messenger or appear itself. Angels, masters and teachers are all messengers for the Creator.

Occupants of the angelic realm take whatever form our belief system holds. If you think angels have wings and halos, this is how they will manifest to you. If you pray to a particular saint, then her/his appearance will be as you visualized.

No one knows for absolute certainty what or how many dimensions there are above earth. As we advance further into this new age, more and more information will be available to us. We *do know* that we are not alone in this Universe.

Like attracts like.
Whatever the conscious mind thinks and believes,
The subconscious identically creates.

Brian Adams, *How to Succeed*

CHAPTER THREE

Thought Forms

TO UNDERSTAND HOW ENTITIES and energies influence us, the effects of vibrational frequencies need to be considered. Thoughts are vibrational frequencies dwelling either inside or outside of our beings. These energies act upon us in many ways, and we are extremely sensitive to the vibrations around us. We are susceptible to and our psyches are wide open to thought forms of all kinds, whether loving, detrimental, positive, negative, thought-provoking, energy draining, soul inspiring, depressing, healing, unhealthy or a host of other sensations. These frequencies can work either **for** or **against** us.

There are three sources of vibrational frequencies. The first, thoughts instilled in our minds from **conscious** and **subconscious** sources, are in turn further influenced by the second, **Universal Frequencies.** The third source external to our physical being emanates from **powerful places** and **objects.** Although they all exist outside of us, each of them has subtle, profound effects on our well being.

To understand how energy initially effects us, we need to have an awareness of the condition of our subtle bodies and aura, and what Universal thoughts we attract. As we will later discover, it is our aura that has the power to attract or repel attacks from unwanted entities.

THE SUBTLE BODIES

Energy fields that have direct impact on our physical well being are called subtle bodies. They are dependent on the condition of our emotional and mental state. The subtle bodies consist of the ETHERIC, EMOTIONAL AND MENTAL bodies (see diagram, Subtle Bodies). The three make up our aura. Individuals whose perception is not bound by three-dimensional thinking can see, feel and sense these fields. Corinthians 15:44 states man has a natural body and a spiritual body.

Etheric

Cocooning our physical self is a force field called the etheric body. It is through its webbing, which radiates about four inches around our body, that conditions from the emotional and mental bodies are filtered into the physical body.

Emotional

The energy field directly outside the etheric and encircling the physical is our emotional body. Happiness, sadness, fears, joy, love, hatred, etc., originate in this area. These emotions are filtered through the etheric which in turn affects the physical body in some overt form. An example of this process would be acquiring a new job, one that will advance your career. Excitement, joy, elation and release from tension may be felt. Physical reactions might cause fluttering in the stomach, smiles and increased vitality and a *joie de vivre*. On the other hand, not getting that job will transmit a message for the physical body to react with a headache, upset stomach or loss of energy.

SUBTLE BODIES

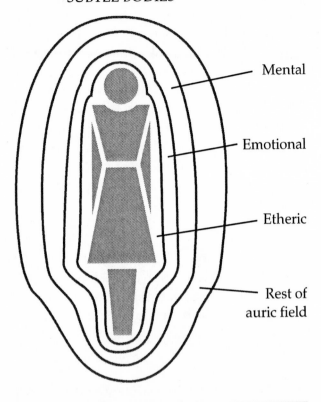

Mental

Emotional

Etheric

Rest of
auric field

Mental

The mental body surrounds the emotional. Prejudice,
intellect, morals, judgment, understanding, and discern-
ment are just a few of the thoughts characteristic of this field.
A situation, such as doing poorly on an exam, triggers a
mental response of judgment against you or the examiner.
This thought filters into the emotional body, causing anger
or unhappiness. These emotions in turn sift through the
etheric webbing causing a physical response of a headache or
other dis-ease.

When thoughts and negative emotions are too difficult for a person to handle, illness can result. The following chart shows how such a chain reaction can occur.

EVENT	MENTAL RESPONSE	EMOTIONAL	PHYSICAL
vacation	compensation for hard work	happiness	increased energy, tension release
death of a loved one	remorse	fear, despair anger	tears, upset stomach, shaking, loss of appetite
argument	judgment	anger	headache, tension
lying	morality self-discipline	depression fear	lack of energy upset stomach

Physical

The physical body is the densest of all the bodies. We know it exists because it can be seen, felt and experienced. It is the last to respond to the emotions and thoughts which originated in the emotional and mental self. This body is also the last to give up and receive any conditions such as headaches, rashes, pains and so on. It traps and selfishly preserves its precious cargo.

AURA

The subtle bodies make up the **aura**, an energy field reflecting the condition of all bodies. It contains vibrational colors, which change according to our emotional and mental conditions. If a situation triggers the emotion of anger, the entire field will change to be a brilliant red. Or, if calmness is felt, the aura will reflect a light blue shading. When no overpowering emotion is currently experienced, the aura reflects colors that correspond with your overall soul direction in this lifetime. It may have some green shades, indicating that you possess healing energies. There may be blue hues for your communication skills, yellow for creativity and so on. The colors and conditions of the chakras can also be discerned in this area.

It is the fragile outer shell, surrounding the aura, that we must learn to protect from undesirable thought forms, entities, human parasites and psychic attacks. In order to do this, we may need to do some internal house-cleaning.

When there is conflict between our conscious and subconscious thoughts, an inner struggle begins. The subconscious, being the stronger, attracts like energy from the Universe and the astral plane. The conscious idea of deserving love, happiness, prosperity and good health will not manifest if the subconscious is retaining the thought that it is unworthy of these positive principles. In such a case, the subconscious has old, preconditioned beliefs from this and even previous lives that are no longer valid. Our blueprint needs to be rearranged and rewritten to release these antiquated convictions.

A personal example of how powerful the subconscious can be at holding old "stuff" is: Until recently I had trouble with self-worth and assertiveness. I unconsciously chose a career and relationships where others were always in control.

As a result, my true Inner Light was terrified of revealing itself for fear of persecution. I was hiding in order to protect myself from being identified by others. Through crystal meditations, healing sessions and past-life regressions, it was discovered that in a previous incarnation I had been a healer and psychic who was tragically burned for my beliefs. A person, whom I had trusted, had turned me over to the authorities.

My soul's blueprint carried this fear of projecting an attitude of power over into this life. With this insight, I began to work on releasing my unworthiness and moved towards finding my inner self. I was also able to reconcile my feelings towards the person who had had me persecuted. In fact, this individual was one of the catalysts who encouraged my quest into the spiritual realm.

Each of us must be willing to look within, to see how we are affecting the condition of our aura. For example, if the thought is held that we want to attract the perfect mate with our subconscious still holding onto the hurt and pain from a previous relationship, it thinks we are unworthy of being loved. Conversely, if there is a strong conviction at all levels of our being that we are worthy and deserve a partner, our actions and responses will reflect this positive self-belief. A new message is released from the subconscious into our aura. We are able to let go of all negative thoughts. Reprogramming occurs. All unworthy suggestions are purged from the subconscious. This transformation of the subconscious permits the conscious to follow suite, so that we transmit one consistent vibrational message.

There are numerous ways harmonious states can be achieved. A few suggestions are using crystals, gemstones, herbal remedies, chakra balancing and a host of other new age techniques.

It is up to each of us to do our own mental housecleaning. With the wonderful energies of Ascension (for more information on this subject refer to Bowman's *Crystal Ascension*) being channeled into this planet at this precise minute, all of us can affect a transformation. By working with the energies of Ascension, we can raise the vibrations of our subtle bodies to higher universal frequencies. Through moving every aspect of our lives into the Light, synchronicity can be achieved with all humankind, the angelic realms, Nature, Masters and life forms. Entities will no longer be feared or misunderstood.

In order to work with the fourth and higher dimensions, we must be aware of how the Universal Frequencies affect our aura.

UNIVERSAL FREQUENCIES

Thoughts flow from above and move down through each plane until they reach our physical bodies. A broad, high-level beam of light, such as planetary healing, originates in the upper spiritual realms. As it filters down through the various layers, it becomes more and more specific until it hits our subtle bodies. Our mental and emotional body will interrupt these filtered thoughts in "human" terminology, and perhaps we are compelled to take an active part in cleaning up our environment. Another example is the following domino effect:

LEVEL	MESSAGE
Spiritual	Message of light
Casual	Humankind to be as one
Astral	Help humanity
Mental	I put aside judgment
Emotional	I am having joy with others
Etheric	All is well
Physical	Increased energy and lessening of pain

By the time the original message of light reaches our dimension, we feel energy and peace with all aspects of life.

Universal thoughts of negative and positive content float around our auras. Those we attract, depend upon the thought forms contained within our auras. Like attracts like. Negative "noise" prevents us from tapping into the Ascension energies. These are thought vibrations expelled into the atmosphere by inhabitants of this planet from their destructive emotions and lower mental thoughts. These negative thoughts are like a thick, dense smog waiting to permeate our personal energy fields. If we also harbor negativity in our thoughts, this floating debris prevents us from rising above everyday situations and achieving the positive aspects of Universal thought. We then become human magnets attracting additional adverse thoughts from the Universe. Because we hold onto an emotion or mental problem, we are the most vulnerable to attacks from other entities or people while caught in these lower frequencies. We fall into the trap of being unable to receive higher spiritual wisdom because we can't rise above the noise. Constant mechanical chatter fills our minds when we wish to turn off the world. Difficulty is experienced when falling asleep, meditating, concentrating on a task, or enjoying leisure time. We have allowed our auras to be inundated with debris that should have been filtered out. The mind needs to reach above this lower distracting energy and tap into the universe's positive frequencies.

Positive energies are there for us to utilize. These Ascension vibrations consist of bands of unconditional love, inspiration, wisdom, higher guidance, and creativity from the Masters and the Creator level. To attract these frequencies, the mind must to be free of negative programming to harmonize with the soul. We need to become clear receivers. We need to be willing to open to new thoughts, sensations, concepts and other planes of activity.

The best of both worlds can be achieved by integrating our thinking process and reprogramming negative thoughts. As in this chapter's example of the difficulty experienced taking my own power and place in this world, we must truly look within and examine how we have been jeopardizing spiritual growth. Ask yourself these questions.

- Do I harbor self-defeating thoughts?
- Do I feel unworthy of receiving from others?
- Do I feel inferior?
- Am I afraid of being alone?
- What am I doing to attract the positive Universal Frequencies?

Any thought whether of a positive or negative nature returns three-fold to the originator.

EXTERNAL VIBRATIONAL THOUGHTS

The last influential type of thought form is the energy existing outside of us. This has no relationship to the condition of our aura. But, we need to be aware of external sources of energy because they have just as profound an affect on our well being as our aura and Universal Frequencies. Their amount of influence is dependent on our internal receiving system. You may be a **kinesthetic, visual or auditory** person. Being a **kinesthetic** person means vibrations are felt and sensed more readily with the body. **Visual** people use their third eye to see into other dimensions, while **auditory** sensors hear inside their heads. Some of us are a combination of all three styles, but mostly one is more dominant than the other.

Science has proven that electromagnetic energy permeates and surrounds our planet. Just as humans have chakra centers, through which energy flows, so does the Earth. Outside of our etheric and subtle bodies are many major and minor meridians where energy crosses and flows. Similarly our planet has several major and minor intersecting points. The spots where these energy grids bisect one another are called ley lines. At such points, we have a number of ancient temples and buildings still standing. Stonehenge and the Great Pyramid of Giza are just two examples of remaining structures built on ley lines.

Certain places, such as ancient temples and sites, hold emotional memories or blueprints of the people who once frequented them. Not only do we pick up others' thought forms, but also our own energy can resonate and empathize as if we are personally experiencing these sensations.

When visiting other ancient temples and pharaonic burial grounds in Egypt, bittersweet emotions surfaced. Uncontrollable tears rolled down my cheeks; my soul was in a lot of pain. I could "hear" the music in the Temple of Hathor and feel the sweat and blood of the tomb builders in the Valley of the Kings. In England, at Canterbury Cathedral I "heard" and "sensed" the chanting of the monks.

Energy affects each of us in different ways. Each locality has certain energy, overall mood or attitude that permeates the area.

We can enter a house, office, store, hotel, church, temple, restaurant or library and feel neither negative vibrations or positive energizing sensations. Chances are, if you have no feelings, you are not consciously aware of existing energies. But, be forewarned some reaction is taking place. You may feel inexplicably angry, be irritable, appear stressed, nervous or perhaps calm. Your reaction will depend on the type of thought form(s) expelled by the person or people who were or are in that building.

Many years ago, I was working as a recruiter for a large company. Due to a recession, we were downsizing. Everyone, from the mail clerks to directors, was apprehensive that their position would be the next to be declared surplus.

It was one of my duties to see terminated employees about their benefits before they left the company. These dehired people understandably were experiencing devastating emotions. Their feelings ran from anger to depression. At that time in my life, I was not aware of the effects of external energies and, like a sponge, soaked up not only the negative feelings of these people but also of the other concerned employees. I suffered from a despondent state of mind every time I thought about work and entered the office building. The vibrations engulfed me like a thick, heavy fog.

Alternatively, we can be in the presence of love, calmness and spiritual healing. Most of us experience a sense of completeness and serenity at a place of worship where vibrations of light and prayer permeate our auras. All those who had previously occupied the edifice had the same mind-set, to be closer to God and nourish their spiritual selves. Communing with Nature can affect healing by revitalizing our minds and bodies. A lake, ocean or running water soothes our vibrations as we absorb Nature's natural healing rays.

Natural settings can have fantastic positive effects on us. One natural power center is the Grand Canyon in the United States. While visiting the amazing phenomena of red rock, I could hear the spiritual resonance of the earth. A low-pitched humming emanating from the rocks instantly cleared my aura of all the unsavory energies encountered in Las Vegas. The panoramic view of miles and miles of red glowing mountains took my breath way. The piñon pine and juniper trees soothed my soul. I had an overpowering sense of coming home again, and for a brief while, I had the sensation of soaring through time and space.

As stated earlier, every person experiences vibrations according to their unique constitution. The form will vary, depending on the way in which we sense these various energies. For instance, if you were to hold a natural quartz crystal, a number of sensations might occur. A visual person could possibly sense colors or symbols flashing through the mind. An auditory sensor might "hear" music or gentle sighs, while a kinesthetic type would sense its power coursing through the body.

One famous crystal guaranteed to elicit a response is the Crystal Skull. It is probably the finest crystal artifact ever discovered, perfectly carved clear natural quartz the shape and size of a human skull with a removable jaw. This crystal was discovered in Belize in 1923 by Anna Mitchell-Hedges, the daughter of F.A. Mitchell-Hedges, a British archaeologist. Anna, sixteen at the time, glimpsed a glass like object jutting out of some rubble at the ruins of an ancient Mayan temple. When the treasure was dug up, the Mayan workers went wild with excitement. Their lost deity had been returned! Many archaeologists, psychics, scientists and antiquities experts have speculated on what people(s) crafted this masterpiece. Frank Dorland, a renowned crystallographer, did extensive work on the Skull. He observed noises, odors, lights and symbols emanating from it. There are many theories as to its origins, ranging from it being stolen from the Holy Lands during the Crusades to the lost civilization of Atlantis. No matter what its origin, there is no question as to its unusual effects on both the subconscious and conscious mind.

When the keeper of the Skull, Anna (a.k.a. Sammy), lived in Kitchener, Ontario, I had the opportunity of visiting this ancient artifact a number of times in 1986. The first time I entered Sammy's living room, I couldn't get over the casual manner in which the Skull was sitting on a coffee table with books and nick knacks surrounding it. It was very much a part of her household. When I commented on this, I was told that the Skull did not wish to be shut away and only revealed at certain times. It needed to be displayed. At a later date, I saw another crystal skull at the London Museum. It was dull and lifeless due to being locked in a case away from human contact.

Upon viewing the Mitchell-Hedges Skull, I initially felt tiny tingles of energy slowly creeping up my arms. Then, a profound, overpowering buzzing noise exploded in my head. Breathing became more rapid. My entire chakra system felt as if being repositioned. My subtle bodies realigned and I felt a deeply entrenched soul memory of coming home. Tears involuntarily rolled down my face. Finally, I experienced a deep calmness. All of these responses took place over a few short minutes, but it felt like a lifetime. Sammy sat knowingly across from me, drawing a picture of a past life she felt I had lived with the Skull. After leaving her home, I experienced over the next few days some memories of having worked with crystals in past lives. From this meeting with the Skull I was guided to write *Crystal Awareness*. Each subsequent time I was with the Skull, I could feel subtle shifts in consciousness. I was more open to accepting my spiritual path and prompted to honor my intuitive self. My life changed in many ways. I left my job as a recruiter. I surrounded myself with hundreds of crystals and began experimenting, healing with and writing about quartz. My focus in life had altered. There was no aspect of my approach to life that was ever the same again.

It is not unusual to be in the presence of something we just can't resist picking up, such as an unusual stone, book or picture. It is as if our hands are itching to touch it. Remembering how each of us senses vibrations, we may see symbols with our inner sight, hear voices, or have a physical reaction to the object. Special people, who can read objects, are psychometrists. The ancients called this art, thaumaturgy. By holding an article such as a ring or watch they can tune into the owner's vibrations. There are tiny memory cells or aka threads scattered over the object. Enid Hoffman, the author of *Huna, A Beginner's Guide*, describes these threads as etheric matter or ectoplasm. Its sticky consistency extends like tiny threads to objects and people to establish a line of communication with them. This bonding begins as early as infancy with a child becoming attached to significant caregivers and toys. When either are removed from the baby's personal field, anxiety sets in and the child cries with distress.

Based on the above psychic bonding, it stands to reason that each of us can be affected, either consciously or subconsciously, by the vibrations of inanimate objects such as jewelry, pictures, books, furniture, clothing, dishes, cars, silverware, etc. Although not as powerful as places on ley lines, these articles can carry positive and negative vibrations that affect our emotional, mental and spiritual well being.

A piece of jewelry obtained as an heirloom or purchased from an antique/used jeweler contains previous owner(s) energies. Their emotional and mental vibrations will have been transferred to the jewelry; they will have sent out aka threads. You will be affected by these factors by wearing this object. It may manifest by slightly altering your emotional responses, such as a sense of sadness, depression, happiness, nervousness or whatever overall vibrations were instilled in the object. If it is a watch from a deceased relative, then you probably will have a good feeling while wearing it. It will bond you to this person's energies. However, if the person was not known to you, chances are, the energies will be foreign and therefore uncomfortable. Whatever your reaction, it is important the jewelry be cleared of the other person's aka threads. (See Chapter 7 for clearing techniques.)

I recently had an unpleasant experience with some artifacts purchased from an auction. I acquired a beautiful assortment of vases and figurines that had had at least two known previous owners, the most recent being a widow who was forced to sell her treasures. While I was unwrapping them and placing them in the living room, I sensed a slight feeling of sadness, which I pushed aside. That night I had foreboding dreams. In the morning, I detected a heaviness permeating the house, which was definitely more pronounced in the direction of the living room. When I entered this area, I saw a thin gray mist hovering around the cabinet holding the vases. I sensed the despair, sadness and grief of this widow having to let go of her valuables. Her energy had definitely spun strong aka threads around her articles. It took me several attempts to rid these energies from the objects and my house.

Vibrations can be imprinted on furniture, houses, cars, books, etc., that are in all probability not compatible with our own. For us to reach into the higher realms of Universal Frequencies we must be able to clear, not only our own undesirable thoughts, but those that emanate from places and things that surround us. As we become more attuned to our spiritual self, we automatically are more sensitive to the power and source of our thoughts. Therefore, it is obvious that it is in our best and highest interests to be very selective of our thoughts. We have the potential of falling prey to unwanted vibrations, entities, psychic attacks and people who feed off our energies.

THOUGHTS ARE LIKE BOOMERANGS

Eileen Cady, *The Dawn of Change*

CHAPTER FOUR

The Veil Is Lifted: How We Attract Entities

NOT ONLY CAN ENTITIES and negative energies be drawn into our auras through thought forms, but invasion can occur from various other channels. The veil, separating the astral plane from the third dimension, can unknowingly be lifted. It can happen while pursuing our spiritual path, having surgery, being involved in an accident, being x-rayed, from a sudden shock, being a sensitive, entering into low vibrational places and a near death situation. Dabbling with occult tools such as ouiji boards, table rapping, tarot cards and out-of-body experiences can induce entity involvement. The death and subsequent mourning of a close relative or friend can encourage visitations from earthbound spirits. The steps to prevent unwanted beings from entering our personal magnetic fields are largely dependent on the entities' reasons for attachment. Entities are neither necessarily negative nor unwanted, but we need to concentrate on selecting only the highest and best possible teachers for our spiritual growth. Therefore, we must become aware of how we are putting ourselves in jeopardy.

THE INITIATE

One viable entrance for an entity intrusion is by seeking higher awareness. The majority of us are novices at entering the spiritual planes. When faced with the challenge of learning how to handle more and more light, we often open up too quickly, without proper protection. We are transforming ourselves into a higher body of light without knowing the precise steps to take. The luxury of being in a closed spiritual society, receiving guidance from seasoned masters, is not feasible. The majority of transformational work is achieved in isolation. Spiritual evolvement is a private, trial-by-error metamorphosis.

Just as we progress from the womb to the tomb through various natural stages of physical, mental and emotional maturing, so do we spiritually. This evolutionary cycle symbolically moves us from infant, through toddler, childhood, adolescence, young adult and senior over a lifetime. It is not possible to remain at one single stage without mental and emotional repercussions. We must move forward and grow spiritually.

When beginning to experiment with mediation, channeling, chakra balancing, flower remedies, crystals and other consciousness-raising tools, we enter an altered realm of existence. With this comes the realization that there are two sides to life: what we see externally in the third dimension, and what is perceived within and beyond. What often happens is that we are not truly in one world or the other; we are alternately somewhere in between. We are out of balance, unable to make decisions. Switching from being a predominately left-brain thinker to the right causes us to lose some of our logical reasoning powers. It becomes easier to "Let the Universe decide." This way, no responsibility is taken. When this message is relayed to family and friends, employers, etc.

who are not on the path, more problems arise. They fear we are either going crazy or are envious of this new-found serene approach to life. There may be a tendency for us to look down upon others not on their path and to discontinue their friendship. We envision ourselves as a 100-watt bulb burning brightly, while everyone else is dimly glowing at a mere 40 watts. Earnestly pursuing heightened awareness makes us not better, but different, from the rest of the population. A natural reaction to all of this is a temporary withdrawal from what is perceived as a conventional lifestyle.

I experience a great deal of isolation from what others perceive as the "normal" way of life. As a child, I felt somewhere deep within that there was a much grander place than earth. I would often be filled with a great sadness and burning desire to return to where I could "hear the angels sing." I was very uncomfortable being in a physical body and was awkward at all activities requiring strength and endurance. In my teens, although I participated in social activities, I still felt an aloneness that nothing outside of me could fill. I lived in this world but was not part of it.

This stage of disinterest in worldly events and having a somewhat passive response may continue for a time. Symbolically we are at the toddler stage, an ego-centered period of development.

We are here on earth to assimilate our energies into third-dimensional life. This is not an easy task. But the message, clearly in having a spiritual awakening, does not mean removing self to some magical kingdom. It is, in fact, a bringing of wisdom and magic into this realm. There must not be a separation of the two worlds but a harmonious blending of the two. While this transformation is taking place, we can get caught between the two, and this is when we are open to entity possession. Being on the path, our aura glows and vibrates with more brightness than average, but working in the light is not a guarantee of automatic protection!

In my late twenties I unknowingly spent time developing myself psychically rather than spiritually. I did many things that caused me to attract a great deal of unwanted energies into my aura. I was like a neon sign flashing VACANT, SPACE FOR RENT. I thought the astral plane was the place to be. And it was only in my thirties when I pursued my spiritual education in full force that I discovered the damage I had done.

Without our knowledge, protection is gone. If there are any holes or tears in our protective shell, undesirable spirits will enter our personal energy fields. Chances are, unless consciously erected protective energies are built up, we are or will be vulnerable.

CHAKRA DISTRESS

(See diagram, Body Chakras, for chakra locations and descriptions.)

When beginning to meditate, doorways open to new and exciting energies. Our personal boundaries dissolve, allowing us to become one with other dimensions. The mind becomes completely disassociated with the body. We are exposed to all energies, of both high and low frequencies. Our upper chakras, third eye and crown, in particular, open and oscillate at new frequencies. This is how we receive communication, not only from our souls but also other dimensions. The remaining chakras may or may not be vibrating at the same rate. It is very common for a person, working on increasing awareness, to have blockages in the lower centers. For instance, an obstructed base chakra is associated with feelings of listlessness, lack of motivation and poor concentration. If untreated, these energy distortions can lead to depression. Also, a person with a dysfunctional base

BODY CHAKRAS

7. **Crown** *Ascension energies, connection to Masters
   (spiritual stagnation)

6. **Third Eye** *intuitive, images, inner Sight
   (blocked visualization, impaired sensitivity)

5. **Throat** *speak your truth
   (blocked expression, stuttering)

4. **Heart** *love energy, soul connection
   (jealousy, hate, inability to give or receive love)

3. **Solar Plexus** *happy, stimulated, power
   (stress, fear, anger)

2. **Spleen** *courage, acceptance, Creativity
   (guilt, overindulgence)

1. **Root** *fully participate in life
   (fatigue, depression, wrapped up in material world)

* open
( ) closed

CHAKRAS IMBALANCE

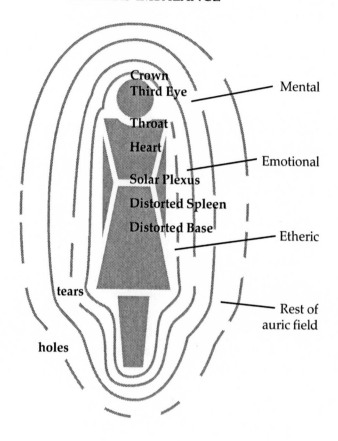

chakra has trouble being "grounded." This means difficulty is experienced when functioning in the physical world. If the next center, the spleen, is obstructed, then creativity and self-confidence are decreased. A poorly opened solar plexus manifests in a lost sense of purpose, resulting in the person not being able to utilize his/her power. With any of these blockages, imbalances occur in the subtle bodies. The Chakra Imbalance sketch will clarify this. Because there is an incongruent distribution, the aura becomes malleable and tiny holes or tears manifest. We are then unable to fend off incoming negative energies.

SURGERY /ACCIDENTAL INJURY

Chakras get out of alignment during any surgical procedure. An invasion to the physical will cause repercussions in the etheric bodies. Having a gall bladder removed or treated with laser will definitely cause a rupture in the spleen and solar plexus chakras. A hysterectomy or prostrate surgery disfigures the base center. Heart operations affect the heart chakra. Careful balancing and healings can be done through crystals, Reiki treatments, flower remedies, radionics and meditation. (Aura sealing techniques are given in Chapter 7).

Anesthetic is guaranteed to soften the aura. All psychic defense systems are removed. While under this drug, the silver cord is still attached to the physical, but we are not in control of our bodies. All those lost souls are waiting to pounce on an anaesthetized body. People often complain that the effects of anesthetic are worse than the operation. Traces can be found in the blood system months afterward, weakening not only the immune system but spiritual defenses as well.

Whenever there is even a minor damage to the body such as a sprained ankle, the aura shifts to accommodate the injury. Because of this slight alteration, we are potentially opening to outside forces. Coupled with a painkiller, the defense level of our protective shield is diminished. Since body parts are linked to the chakras, the corresponding chakra will be out of alignment. The degree of imbalance will depend on the type and severity of the injury. For instance, spinal injuries to the coccyx or disk areas are linked to the lower chakras. This is a message from soul that we are focusing too much on the physical aspects of life. Some of that energy needs to go into the spiritual.

The following chart will help associate some body parts to chakras.

INJURY/DISEASE AREA	ASSOCIATED CHAKRA
Feet, ankles, legs, coccyx, hips	base
Sexual organs	spleen
Stomach, abdomen, pancreas	solar plexus
Lungs heart	heart
Tonsils	throat

X-RAYS

X-rays destroy the aura 's electromagnetic force field. Radiation weakens the outer shell making us vulnerable to negative energies. Also, passing through security devices such as metal detectors in airports cause tiny holes and tears in our auric field.

SUDDEN SHOCK

A sudden shock of a profound emotional nature can cause our energy system to go haywire, which opens it to entity entrance. Just hearing the news, that someone close has died, jars all chakras out of balance. An experience such as whiplash, where there is no overt physical injury, can damage the subtle bodies. Unexpected loss of employment does the same. Divorce or separation, whether self or partner initiated, shocks the emotional and mental bodies because the end of a love affair is always devastating. The attachment to the other person was through the etheric and lower chakra centers, and it is painful when the aka threads are severed. Childbirth causes a misalignment and shock to both mother and child. The mother has been shielding and protecting the fetus for nine months. Then suddenly a part of her is ripped away and the umbilical cord, the lifeline, is cut. The baby, who has been softly enveloped in embryonic fluid deep within the sanctity of the mother's aura, now must survive without all of her energies.

BEING A SENSITIVE

Spirits can invade the energy fields of people who have a naturally sensitive and vulnerable nature. If you seek harmony, are romantic, enthusiastic, warm, communicative, compassionate, nurturing, searching for self and spirituality, then you are a prime target. Being overly sympathetic to others' problems opens you up to taking on their energies.

My mother suffers with an eye affliction called macular degeneration. With the disease's progression, I share her distress and anger. When a colleague of mine developed a similar problem, I was naturally sympathetic. I did not realize that, because I resonated so deeply with these two women's problems, I had attracted an entity into my aura. This discarnate also had an eye disease. My naturopath, who subsequently removed the energy, discovered the being. I had no idea I was even invaded! Looking back, I can see how my personality made me susceptible to the entity along with holding fear that the same affliction would strike me. So, the combination of my caring and fear allowed this spirit to manifest in my energy field. It fed off my sympathy which would appear in the astral plane as a glowing, welcoming, soft light. My solar plexus and heart were wide open.

Being a sensitive is not a punishment; we just have to be more careful about our auric shield and the depth of involvement in others' problems. We need to learn empathy and compassion rather than taking on the energy of the sufferer.

LOW VIBRATIONAL PLACES

There are many locations containing powerful energies that are not conducive to higher vibrations. They hold negative memories, blueprints of emotional events. Even if there are no tears or holes in our personal energy fields when we are in the vicinity of a location where there has been a disaster of great emotional and mental trauma, these energies are strongly experienced by us.

London Tower caused me to shiver with dread and apprehension. The souls of tortured prisoners hung in every dark nook and cranny; horror had been absorbed into the stone walls. I could sense the vibrations of pain and agony.

My stepson was on a trip to Pennsylvania with a group of architectural students. He called to say he had just visited the area where the Battle of Gettysburg had fought. When I inquired as to what he felt, he said it was as if he could actually see and feel the battle taking place. Fear and death shrouded the area.

In such circumstances, entities are not picked up in the aura, rather their emotions are felt as "astral garbage." In all probability the majority of spirits who left traces of these horrible deaths, have moved on. But, the memories of suffering have permeated the locations of the London Tower and the battlegrounds. After leaving such a place, we may feel depressed, suffer a headache, or be in a reflective mood for a few hours or days. The intensity with which it affects an individual will vary.

Hospitals are a prime holding area of emotional and physical negative discharge. Earthbound entities are just waiting to invade the living! Many people die in hospitals and do not travel on to the light because they are frustrated, in shock and denial. Whether we are a visitor or patient, we are viewed as potential hosts. Ironclad protection is needed. If you are a kinesthetic person, the atmosphere in a hospital feels heavy and oppressive. If a visual sensitive, you might see swirling masses of grey grids or the actual spirits. If an auditory sensor, it is an inharmonious noise. Doctors' offices and clinics have similar, yet less, intense vibrations.

Burial grounds are another source of negativity. Extra protection is needed if attending a funeral or just visiting. The ground soaks up the mournful pain of the living as well as the dead. Again, many spirits hover around their bodies because they are afraid and don't know enough to go to the light. And we, being the living and on our spiritual path, are natural targets.

The dead do not like to be disturbed. I grew up in a house that harbored strange energies. It was not unusual to have lights flick on and off. Doors would open. Creaks and groans were nightly occurrences. We were the first owners of the home so these disturbances could not be attributed to antiquated wiring and structural problems. I had a dreadful fear of one particular bedroom where my sister and I would often feel many eyes watching us even with the curtains closed.

We both suffered from nightmares when sleeping in this part of the house. Recently it was discovered that the house had been built on the edge of an Indian burial ground. Our theory is the Indians were very angry we were on their sacred ground. I sensed that they couldn't physically harm us, but they sure played havoc with our fears.

Entities inhabit bars and gambling establishments. It is so important that we have our protection working full time in such places. If you have ever had "a night out on the town" where you had too much to drink, then you probably brought a few entities back home with you. The next day, not only is a hangover suffered, but your aura has a lot of extra weight to it. You really feel out of sorts, with a heaviness in body and mind, blaming it on the booze. These entities usually leave after a few hours when they discover you are not going to respond to their needs of additional drinking. They return back to the bars and wait for the next host.

NEAR-DEATH EXPERIENCES (N.D.E.)

Due to modern resuscitation equipment, more people are revived from actual death and are sharing their incredible experiences. Many, who have had a near-death experience, relate that entities of various levels were encountered while their consciousness was separated from their physical body. Some commonalties are: floating above the physical body, going into a tunnel which leads to a bright light, the presence of deceased loved ones, meeting with guardian angels, and a disappointment at coming back from the light into the body. One well known account of such a N.D.E. is Betty Eadie's book, *Embraced by the Light*.

Betty was in hospital hooked up to life support systems when she felt consciousness leave her body. With the realization that she was dead, three spirit monks appeared. They telepathically removed her anxiety. She later went through the tunnel and met a personality with an illuminating, golden aura whom she identified as Jesus. When she returned to her body, terrifying beings surrounded her. She felt these entities were going to kill her, until a light poured into the room, dispersing them. In all probability, she was connecting with all the astral garbage that would be floating around the hospital. This debris would take on the form of monstrous spirits. Eadie's meeting with Christ would manifest because of her Christian background. To Christians, the Son of God would be the natural spirit to meet as He represents salvation. The Buddhists would hold Buddha as the highest, the Jews, God, and the Muslims, Allah.

Helene Laura Ampell, who is associated with Dr. Frank Alper's Adamis Enterprises in Phoenix, Arizona, had some similar experiences. Although her N.D.E. took place nearly 35 years ago, she says it as just as vivid, having the same emotional impact as if it had happened yesterday. The following is Helene's account.

In 1962, I went into the hospital to give birth to my second child. As my first was a "C" section, the same procedure was presumed for this child.

On entering the hospital, instead of being sent to a room, I was taken to the labor floor. Before I knew what was happening, an epidermic needle was injected into my back. I desperately tried to fight off the effects of the opiate. This certainly was not how I had my first "C" section. I began to lose control of my extremities and became very short of breath. The hospital staff noticed I was in trouble and began to revive me. I had my first cardiac arrest (I had 4 or 5 over the course of this terrifying time). The head doctor announced his shift was up and left me in the hands of a resident doctor. I had more attacks during his presence and then he left for dinner.

As I felt another seizure coming on, I screamed, "Please dear God, help me. I can't breathe." I grabbed for the oxygen apparatus. In my haste, the tank rolled on its side, clanking against the bed. The noise alerted a passing resident. Code RED hit the P.A. system.

During the time the team was working to revive me, I felt myself high above the bed. I saw the doctors pounding on my chest and administer a needle directly into the heart. An incubator was rolled into my room and a Rabbi or Priest, whomever was nearby, was sent for. My bed was then pushed into the middle of the room and the tube containing the epidermal was disconnected.

As all of this was going on, I was in tremendous turmoil. What was happening to me and what about my baby?

Then, all of a sudden a former boyfriend took my hand. He had died of Bulbar polio when I was 16 years old. The same feelings I had of being overwhelmed by his tenderness and broad smile when we were young returned and intensified. My feelings were transformed into pure love. My deceased Grandmother took my hand as he walked away from me without looking back. Before I could call out to him, my Grandmother said, "It is not your time, my baby. Go back towards the light." Although the peaceful comfort and joy I had upon seeing these special people overwhelmed me, they did not return the same sentiments. Grandmother walked forward with me and I found myself back looking down and hearing these words, "I am losing her, get ready to take the baby."

It was at this point that I remember sliding back into my body. I grabbed for the sheet that was partially covering my body. I was so cold, already missing the glowing warmth from the other side. I heard the nurse cry, "She's alive. Thank you, God!"

I later found out a Priest had given me Last Rites and my unborn child as well. The Rabbi came to my room the next day and said a Blessing to ward off entities and deny them permission to enter our bodies.

My son was finally born. The above events left me with a stutter. When conversing with people, any interruption would cause me to lose my train of thought and I never remembered what I was about to say. All of this lasted for about one year and I truly thought I didn't have long to live. This was not so.

Previous to Helene's N.D.E. she was not on her spiritual path. In later years, when sharing this experience with other lightworkers, she was reassured that others had encountered similar occurrences. It had been very difficult for Helene to discuss her N.D.E. with those who were not pursuing higher awareness. She now has no reservations talking to anyone about her incredible journey.

TESTS OF FAITH

We often cause possessions to come to us when attempting to tap into the other realms of existence. The veil is lifted on the lower parts of the astral plane, through dabbling with the occult: Ouiji boards, table tappings, automatic writing, tarot readings and out-of-body experiences. These are some of the mediums that, when used improperly, attract lower entities.

Ouiji boards were popular when I was in my early teens. A group of girlfriends and I would innocently ask the board to spell out our future husbands' names. We would hold mock seances and request the names of ghosts. Each of us would accuse the others of deliberately moving the pointer around the board.

On reflection, I realize we were playing with fire. We were completely ignorant of the danger in our actions.

Lower entities were being contacted. They were undoubtedly lined up, waiting to have some fun at our expense. To this day, I do not know what the repercussions were. Maybe those spirits are still attached to the rooms we played in.

Table tapping was very in vogue in the United States during the 1840s. The Fox sisters of Hydesville, New York *(The Encyclopedia of Ghosts and Spirits,* 1992), became renowned for their unique methods of spirit communication. The girls claimed to hear unexplained tapping noises in their home. A neighbor helped trace the sounds to an entity that rapped once for "yes" and "twice" for no. They found that this ghost had died in their house five years previously by having his throat slashed. The sisters continued their occult experiments. They began to hold seances. The spirits with which they communicated spoke through rapping on the séance table. This type of "entertainment" caused a wave of spiritualism to erupt in North America and Europe.

I naively tried to contact spirits through table tapping and raising. My family had a cottage in Northern Ontario and I knew that being in close proximity to water would increase psychic force fields. Author Colin Wilson's research *(Poltergeist,* 1981) on dowsing shows that bodies of water have the capacity to record human emotions and imprint these on the surrounding land. My partner and I had that table moving and tapping within minutes. It was quite a phenomenon. I was really excited about the spirit Charlie who communicated with us. In my mind and through knocks, he told us he had died over 400 years ago by the lake. From that night on, until I was able to send him to the light, our ghost remained in residence, causing creaks and groans in the cottage. A heavy depressive atmosphere prevailed. I had innocently conjured up an unwelcome guest.

Automatic writing is another potential medium to attract low-level entities. Unless one is one hundred percent certain the aura is sealed and your thoughts are high enough to channel only the best and highest spirits, lower ones will be attracted and try to communicate. There are so many souls "dying" to communicate with us.

When first opening up, I would patiently sit for set periods of time allowing the energy to push my pen across the page. Some scribbles and unintelligent words would sometimes be made. It was only later when I learned how to safely channel spirit energies that I began to have a writing relationship. (See Chapter 8, "Shedding Light on Darkness.")

There are many directly channeled works written with highly evolved entities guiding the pen. The writer provides the vehicle for the spirit's ideas to be expressed. Jane Roberts is one of the many well-known writers who had a working relationship with the spirit Seth. Together they wrote volumes.

Psychics often contact spirits through divination aides, such as Tarot cards. The experienced reader knows how to extract esoteric wisdom, past, present and future events. The novice needs to be careful and protected in order to avoid contact with the playful, lower entities associated with such cards.

When I was opening up psychically (as opposed to spiritually) I obtained a deck of Tarot cards. When I casually mentioned that I was studying this ancient fortune telling method, my friend, who was more experienced with the astral plane, grabbed the cards. She began blowing on them and repeated a prayer. I was very annoyed with this behavior and never shared my tarot experiences again with her. As I began to write this book, I clearly saw her reasons. She was concerned about the lower entities and thought forms that would be attracted to the cards. Now I understand why I received so much misinformation!

Another way of encountering entities is through out-of-body experiences. O.B.E. is the process of astral travelling. Just as with anaesthetic, there is a strong possibility of entity invasion. While the astral/spiritual body is travelling, all kinds of entities will be encountered.

When I first experimented with O.B.E., it took several tries before my consciousness released. I felt a mixture of fear and excitement each time I prepared myself. When I finally succeeded, a strange floating sensation engulfed me. It did not occur to me to ask for protection or what the end result of astral travel might be. I hovered over my body. Suddenly, my room was filled with numerous dark shapes and I saw (instead of my usual "feeling") grotesque shapes of strange beings with hostile faces. This shocked me back into my body. I was extremely frightened by the experience and decided to not try an O.B.E. again. However, because of this fear, I must have held the spirits like a magnet. The next night as I drifted between sleep and wakefulness, I suddenly felt a crushing weight on my chest before I was unwillingly pushed from my feet by a force that flung me out of my body. I was absolutely powerless to stop the process. I was astrally thrown about the bedroom. A lamp and books were knocked to the floor. I recall screaming the Lord's Prayer and calling on the archangels to cease this invasion. By invoking the light, I was returned to my body and was once again in control. It was definitely a learning experience. It was not until several years later that I felt capable of risking another O.B.E.

EXCESSIVE GRIEVING

Confucius said, "Bemoan not the departed with excessive grief. The dead are devoted and faithful friends; they are ever associated with us." When we excessively grieve for a loved one, we anchor them to this dimension. Because we are in so much pain over losing them, their soul is not free to move on. A lengthy grieving time is unhealthy for both griever and grieved. We are, in fact, selfishly delaying the other's growth.

A friend of the family lost her teenage son in a car accident. Naturally, she was devastated and had a difficult time letting go of him. Due to overwhelming grief, she was unable to focus on the rest of her family and job. She had a nervous breakdown and could not seem to pick up the pieces of her life. She finally visited a medium who was able to communicate with her son. He gently explained how she had been holding him earthbound since his death. He could not go on and do what his soul needed to because he was afraid to leave her alone. After this session, the mother was able to release her son and get on with her life and he with his progression.

THE VEIL IS LIFTED

Part of our spiritual progression is to acknowledge the various levels of existence; the veil is lifted. We become aware of all the ways to attract spirits into our personal energy fields. By understanding the entities' motives and how our 'selves' have been placed in jeopardy, we can start removing and preventing further unwanted intrusions.

If you attack apparent negativity with Negativity,
You merely feed and inflame the source.
It's always best to take the positive in
any conflict.

John and Lynn St. Clair Thomas
Eyes of the Beholder

CHAPTER FIVE

Lost Souls
and Attacks

ALONG WITH THE POTENTIAL COMPLICATIONS of attracting undesirable thought forms, there are dimensions above the physical plane containing vibrational energies that have the possibility of affecting our well being. The three categories of such energies are **discarnate beings, human parasites, and psychic attacks.**

Parasites and attacks originate and are sustained in the fourth dimension. They are negative thought forms generated by humans. Discarnates or ghosts also reside on this level. These lost souls are people who have died, are being held in the astral plane, and can attach themselves to both our auric fields and earth for a variety of reasons.

Spirits surround us! Some people are tuned into them, while others are not consciously aware of their existence. A 1996 Gallup Poll revealed 30% of the population believe in the existence of ghosts. Ghosts may visually materialize or make their existence noticeable through noises, odors and temperature changes.

A renowned healer and metaphysician (Greg Nolan) once confided that he would go into a supermarket and see all the guides, entities and negative thought forms surrounding each customer in the store. Coupled with energy patterns he visualized around the fresh produce, he had a difficult time concentrating on selecting groceries. A woman psychic, Helen Maine of Toronto, a meditation class instructor at Britten Memorial Church in Toronto, told our class of the time she visited her brother who had just purchased an old house. She was relaxing in the bathtub when a group of spirits surrounded her. They were so excited to finally have someone to converse with that she had to tell them to go away until her bathing was completed.

GHOST/DISCARNATE SPIRITS

The first and most noted entity is commonly referred to as a ghost or discarnate being. These are deceased persons who, for one reason or another, are still attached to the third dimension, having not yet reached the higher realms. They are trapped on the astral plane without a physical form. The essence/personality of the dead person has remained, its soul having not yet discarded its earthy personality, thereby delaying its evolution.

The reasons for ghosts are as numerous as the spirits themselves. One universal reason for spirits being earth-bound is they simply were not prepared to die. They had no warning, having drowned, been in a car crash or murdered. Their attention is focused on unfinished business and loose ends. There may be an overwhelming concern with property settlement or distribution of money. A murdered person will stay close to the murderer until justice is administered, or if sudden death occurs through an accident or murder, the victim may be confused, not realizing s/he is dead. Suicides result in earth-bound spirits. They have taken their lives before it was time. Such entities are held in the astral plane for further soul growth and development.

Other souls get trapped in the astral plane if they were overly obsessed with third-dimensional activities. While on earth, a person may have prioritized his/her possessions over all else. For instance, such people might have only focused on the physical aspects of life. They may have had an overly obsessive drive for making money, acquiring possessions, power or sex to such a degree that all energies were channeled in this direction at the expense of making friends, close relationships, a family or pursuing their spirituality. This overwhelming attachment to earthly pursuits is not released at death. Such persons are held in the third dimension, the lower part of the astral plane.

A gambler, drug addict or alcoholic is too addicted to earthly pleasures to move on. Such souls have a compulsion to satisfy their addictions by trying to possess a living person's energies who has the same pursuit in life.

Places of gambling, such as racetracks and casinos, are extremely populated with low-life energies. They impact visitors' magnetic fields, lowering overall vibrations. The serious players are not playing for fun; they are playing because of a driving necessity. Nothing will deter them from their addiction. The spirits around them intensify their highs and lows.

Entities are even attracted to people who smoke. If their addiction was so strong that they literally can't live without their nicotine, then these souls will enter into the auras of smokers. They also get high from the tobacco! Drug abusers also attract the same type of entities, i.e. those who still feel so attached to the physical plane that they crave cocaine or heroin. Alcohol is also a big enticement. When a person drinks too much, the aura softens, becoming malleable. There are a number of spirits hanging around bars waiting to step into a body and taste the liquor. Depending on the host's addictive level and personality, that person may bring home a whole group of beings after a night of drinking. The entity or entities may or may not decide to stick around.

There are also some spirits who fear they will go to hell because of their earthly deeds. This belief holds them in the lower planes until they can be shown that it is necessary and safe to move on.

POLTERGEISTS

Just as there are good and bad persons on earth, there are good and bad entities. Evil spirits are better known as poltergeists. Instead of being drawn to a place, these specters seem to be lured to a particular individual. It is believed they are composed of an energy cluster. They can be "astral garbage," which is a coagulation of negative thought forms or a group of very angry spirits joined together. Whatever their source, poltergeists can be malicious and frightening.

HUMAN ENERGY FORMS

Entities do not have to be in the form of ghosts or poltergeists. They can be generated by people on this plane in two ways. The first is less obvious than the second but just as detrimental. They emanate from people with a strong, controlling personality. The second is from those who seek to psychically harm others.

HUMAN PARASITES

Since this type of energy affront can occur over an extended period of time, the victim is not always aware of being assaulted.

At one time or another, all of us have been in the presence of someone who drains our energy. After leaving such an individual, we feel tired and listless, as if our very life force had been drained away. In most cases, these people are not aware of being a human parasite or what is sometimes referred to as a human vampire. They suck out our energy by unconsciously attaching themselves to our energy system. We become their human batteries; they become charged while we discharge. These vampires put out etheric tentacles which attach to the weakest part of our aura. (See Human Vampire.)

It might be our solar plexus, base center, throat, heart or spleen center that is attacked. These people talk excessively about themselves, rarely giving their audience a chance to respond. They have extremely poor listening skills and tend to be very "I" centered. In other words, ego dominates the conversation.

PSYCHIC ATTACK

The final negative energy generated by people is called psychic attack. It can be unconsciously or deliberately perpetrated. This invasion is from those who overpower others with their strength of will. They are power hungry and very needy. Just as small children feed off the love and attention of parents in order to survive and grow, these people siphon energy from those who have a more passive approach towards life. Advantage is taken of weaker people, and they agree to things they normally wouldn't. For instance we often feel obliged to go somewhere or do something that we do not want to do just to please the other person. Our identity gets pushed aside to permit these people to fulfill their own needs. The dominant person may not even be aware of his/her influence. They will take control of a situation and sway an entire group to their point of view.

In relationships, there is often a stronger person who drains the weaker's energies. Relationships between two adults should ideally be based on unconditional love with each partner having equal status and autonomy. The bonding should nourish each person's spiritual growth, facilitating both to higher consciousness. But, this is not always the case. Problems arise when, instead of the 'best' coming out, the worst side of one or both parties is emphasized. This type of relationship zaps one or both people of energy and individuality. Abuse, whether physical or mental, is occurring. One is submissive, the other dominant. The victim slowly feeds the stronger one. In the case of husband beating a wife, he is the vampire. She is left depleted and convinced the abuse is somehow due to her own shortcomings. She not only is damaged physically but psychically as well. The same occurs with mental cruelty. One spouse deliberately tries to control the other's actions in order to feel important and in charge. Or, one mate tries to change the other, instead of realizing only one's self can be changed. The victimized partner in abusive relationships has given away her/his power. Not only is she damaging her solar plexus center, but in the process opens up to entity attachments.

The next type of attack is a deliberate force from one person to another. Dion Fortune, in her book *Psychic Self Defense,* cites many cases and incidents of psychic attack. In one particular incident a group of occult students directed their avenging energies on a woman who was trying to destroy each of them. She experienced a variety of sensations such as ongoing nightmares, nonmedical based illnesses, suicidal tendencies and neurotic behaviors. It was only after repeated attacks that the woman got the message to leave the group alone.

To comprehend the power of a psychic attack, it can best be explained by studying the effects of a completely opposite force, a healing group. When people gather together to pray for another person's recovery, a very powerful energy is generated. All of us have practiced creative visualization where we "see" ourselves in that new job, attracting the right mate or driving a new car. We have the inner belief and faith that our projected thoughts can alter reality. This same mind set is transferred to healing. Many religious and metaphysical groups have a pre-arranged time when its members consciously project healing energies to a person or specific situation to be healed. All of us are thought generators, and when united with others having the same mind thought, we can effect a healing. We concentrate on the person/situation and see it with our third eye so that the person is clearly visualized as being in perfect health and harmony. What is in fact happening is that the group has created a perfect vision of this person on the astral plane. The subconscious picks up these healthy thoughts and transfers the message to the subtle bodies. Psychic attacks work on the same principal. If a single person or group wishes to harm another, they fill their entire being with thoughts of hate and rage. These destructive energies are projected into the astral plane and surround the aura of the victim. They can also summon up the dark entities to attack their victim as well.

SUMMARY

There are many reasons why entities are attracted to the confines of the third dimension. They are not prepared to die, have a strong desire to be connected to their old life, and seek revenge. We therefore need to be aware of how we attract entities, how to ascertain when these invading energies are present, and finally how to get rid of them.

CHAPTER SIX

The Intruders: The Good, the Bad and the Ugly

As we begin to increase our discerning skills and move further into the light, it is important to know the signs of entity intrusions from **possessions, ghosts, poltergeists, places, psychic attacks, human parasites, astral garbage and karmic entities.**

We must know if our energy is being subjected to undesirable entities or thought forms. Although not everyone will experience the presence of energy in the same manner, i.e. kinesthetic, auditory or visual perception, in some cases, all of the senses will be actively involved with the invading energy.

It is highly unlikely an invasion will occur from more than one type of energy at a time. For instance, the presence of an apparition sensed by prickles on the skin or a cold area in a room will not cause any havoc. It is simply a lost soul and not connected with any other source of intrusion. An evil or ugly entity desirous of revenge makes its presence known through noises, odors or the hurling of objects.

In rare cases, it is possible for more than one entity or energy to be attached to our aura simultaneously. This type of attack is dependent on any physical/emotional/spiritual conditions that may weaken the aura's resistance and the tenacity of the invading spirits.

The possible signs of energy intrusion from **good, bad** or **ugly** sources are listed below, in no particular order of intensity. A symptom is given along with the probable intruding energy source or sources.

1. Sudden mood changes from high to low, especially noticeable in children with temper and behavior problems. **Possession**
2. Hearing voices that tell you what to do or give negative suggestions, i.e., you are no good, you are fat, push on the gas pedal real hard, take the knife and stab him. **Possession**
3. Any uncharacteristic behaviors such as compulsive gambling, excessive drinking, food cravings, sexual needs, buying sprees etc. **Possession**
4. Problems with short-term memory, i.e., forgetting where you placed things, missing keys, objects that you know were there a minute ago. **Possession, Human Parasite, Psychic Attack**
5. Depression for no apparent reason. **ALL ENERGIES**
6. Unexplained blackouts—complete loss of conscious memory for seconds or longer. **Possession, Poltergeist, Places, Astral garbage**
7. Pains that have no physical source. **ALL ENERGIES**
8. Unexplained bruises or marks on your body. **Possession, Poltergeist**
9. Sudden phobias such as a fear of going outside the home, fear of answering the telephone, fears that were not present in your life before. **Possessions, Poltergeist, Psychic Attacks, Human Parasites**
10. Significant weight gain or loss. **Possession, Poltergeist, Psychic Attack, Human Parasites.**

11. Feeling out of sorts. **ALL**
12. Anxiety attacks. **ALL**
13. Draining sensation or bleeding of the chakras. **Possession, Psychic Attack, Human Parasite**
14. Lack of self-esteem. **Psychic attack, human parasite**
15. Sudden difficulty being with other people who are loving and nurturing. **Psychic Attack, Human Parasites**
16. Cold spots in the house. **Ghost, Poltergeist**
17. Nightmares that have a recurring theme. **All**
18. Smelling bad odors. **Ghosts, poltergeists**
19. Sensations of things crawling over your skin. **Ghosts, Poltergeists**
20. Unexplained creaks and groans in a building. **Ghosts, Poltergeists**
21. Closed doors opening. **Ghosts, Poltergeists**
22. Interference on TV screens, electrical equipment. **Ghost, Poltergeist**
23. Spontaneous O.B.E. **Possession.**

This list is in no way complete but will help the reader to ascertain whether there is a possible invasion.

POSSESSIONS

Possessions refer to spirits taking over human minds and bodies. The degree of possession can vary. **Edith Fiore** in her book, *The Unquiet Dead*, cites several case studies of the varying degrees of possession. She states if there is a drug or alcohol addiction, the person will have more than one attacker.

Dr. Carl Wickland in *Thirty Years Among the Dead* dealt with patients who had possessions, displaying such classic behaviors as multiple personalities, blackouts, disorientation and compulsive actions.

The "taking over" can be for a specific period of time as is the case with channelers (see Chapter 8).

The ancient Greeks believed the Gods possessed the bodies of men in order to carry out earthly deeds. Homer was often empowered by the Gods in order to battle negative forces.

The Bible cites many examples of demonic possession. "Jesus gave his disciples powers to cast out destructive spirits" (Matt. 10:1). In Luke (9:49), John said, "We saw on casting out devils in thy name."

Later in fifteenth-century France, Joan of Arc claimed to be possessed by the spirit of the Archangel Michael who guided her to drive out the invading English.

In the medical field, psychiatrists treat multiple personalities. Two well-known cases are Sybil who had seventeen possessions and Eve with three. Each of these women was not consciously aware of the possessing entities.

Jose Pedro de Freitas, the surgeon with the rusty knife, was a poor, illiterate Brazilian. He was possessed by a Doctor Fritz, a German surgeon, who died during World War I. This entity took over Jose in 1955, using his mind and body to perform surgery with a common kitchen knife. There are many documented cases of Jose executing amazing feats of surgery in Brazil. Apparently he spoke to his patients using a heavy German accent. The entity entirely took over a person to perform a service to others *(Reader's Digest,* 1973, p. 144).

Present-day possessions are the djinns or zar spirits, which occur in some factions of Middle Eastern society. These playful spirits are partial to attacking married women with health and emotional problems. Djinns demand that the victims get jewelry, food, clothing and other material comforts before they will depart. A shechah-ez-zar (female priest) removes these invading spirits during a special ceremony. Sacred rites and dances are performed while the victim swirls around until she faints. Her collapse means the djinn have left her body.

THE PRESENCE OF GHOST

Not everyone sees ghosts with his or her physical eyes. Their presence, for the majority, is just an inner sensing. Ghostly appearances can be either comforting or menacing.

THE GOOD

While grieving someone who died a natural death (not murdered), it is common for that ghost to visit certain loved ones before leaving the earth's energies. This person may actually speak or try to communicate in a non-verbal manner. Its presence can be in the form of an odor particular to that person when alive, such as a perfume, cologne, pipe or cigar smoke. It is a gentle, nonthreatening interchange from the other side. The persons these ghosts visit are not frightened by their presence and often welcome them. The deceased person just wants to comfort their loved ones. For instance, a woman from Florida called Mimi had communications with her deceased husband. He had drowned after diving off a boat and striking his head on the swim platform. Mimi sensed his comforting presence for a number of years until one day he came saying, "Mimi, I am saying good-bye. I am moving on to a higher plane." She never felt him near again.

This same type of amiable ghost will often make its presence known to comfort a loved one long after it should have left for higher dimensions. In times of extreme emotional, mental, spiritual and/or physical stress, these beings will alert their loved ones through a thought, smell, symbol or sign. They can stay around for years watching over their children and spouses.

Even if their presence hasn't been felt, ghosts can suddenly materialize as a warning of a pending death. A long deceased parent will often appear to guide and assist children and relatives to the other side. In my mother's case, it was her sister, Jean, who died several years ago. For the first few months after her passing, my mother felt her presence. Then one day, it was gone. Just before my mother's brother's death, Jean began reappearing in Mother's dreams. When my uncle died, Jean was his 'angel' guiding and directing his soul to the light. She subsequently left the third dimension.

Another example of a harmless apparition happened some ten years ago while my mother was arranging flowers in the local Anglican Church during the weekday in preparation for the Sunday services. Her attention was drawn to the altar. Hovering above it was a clearly defined cloudlike shape. As she watched in fascination, the ghost drifted toward the vestry door and passed through it. Mother walked up the center aisle to verify the vestry door was really closed. It was. She had no sense of fear. She felt she had intruded on the entity's time of prayer.

Sylvia Fraser's book, *The Quest For the Fourth Monkey*, cites many examples of sons and husbands who appeared to their wives and mothers to relay messages just before being killed in the war. These women had their men appear in dreams or just before falling asleep.

Deceased spirits often return to give the living messages. A renowned story of such a case involved Dante Alighieri. When he died in 1321, sections were apparently missing from *The Divine Comedy*. His sons frantically searched their father's house for months without recovering the lost papers. Finally, Dante appeared as an apparition and led them to a secret hiding place. The manuscript was found *(Reader's Digest,* 1973, p. 144).

A more recent ghost story concerns an English woman, Dorothy Eady. As a child in England she was intrigued by ancient Egypt and befriended Sir E.A. Wallis Budge, the famous Egyptologist. Dorothy was obsessed by pharaohonic history after recalling a past life in this era, 3,000 years ago. She was the favorite of Pharaoh Sety and had committed suicide in order not to betray him. At the age of 14, he appeared as an apparition to her.

Dorothy married an Egyptian student and moved to Cairo in 1933.

It was after the birth of her son, whom she named Sety, that she began having frequent encounters with the long deceased Pharaoh. He told her about their lives together and how each of them died. Other people saw this figure around Dorothy. She later left her husband and moved to the village of Abydos where in a past life she had been a young temple priestess. This entity guided Dorothy throughout her lifetime. It was a love story that defied time (Cott, 1987).

More recently and closer to home, there is a renowned house owned by a couple, Harvey and Lois, in small theatrical town in Ontario. The presence of the woman's father, Jake, is often felt in this house. Lois's dad passed away several years ago. He loved his house and daughter above all else and appears to be the guardian of both.

Jake made his presence known to his daughter when she moved back into the family house. She knew it was her dad by the strong scent of his tobacco smoke, which was apparently the cause of his death (lung cancer). Lois never actually sees Jake; she only senses his presence when he is attracted to what is taking place in and around the house, as in times of family crisis or when something occurs to make him joyful.

Harvey actually sees his father-in-law materialize. Jake helps Harvey arrange and plant flowers through mental suggestions in their lush water garden. He speaks to Harvey in times of extreme stress when his daughter is involved. Lois never feels her father when away from the property, but feels that if she were in trouble Jake would be there.

It was obvious, from my visit with this couple, that Jake's house and family was indeed being well cared for. As part of a tour of the house, I was shown a guest bedroom. When the door opened, I was overcome by a pressing, tightening sensation on my chest. My breathing became labored.

My first response to my host was to blurt out, "Someone died in here." I did not fear or sense a heavy presence in the room, just a pressure on my lungs and heart. I carried this feeling with me for the time I remained in the house. I discussed the possible origin of this intrusive energy with Lois and Harvey, but we could not come up with any plausible explanations. It was only after further interviewing Lois a couple of weeks later that I was able to discern what caused the shortness and tightness of breath. I had picked up on the presence of Jake. The physical symptoms in my chest were similar to what he would have suffered with lung cancer.

This same house also has a friendly ghost in the garden. This fellow is seen by Harvey. He describes him as about five feet tall wearing a pullover type hood and high laced boots. Harvey believes he is about 200 years old. The reason for him being outside the house is to attend the garden. The apparition guides Harvey in planting trees, flowers and in taking care of the property. The house has inside and outside spirits and both are welcomed by the owners.

THE BAD

Not all ghosts have quiet, loving, protective natures. The "bad"' or menacing spirits frighten us by manifesting as unfriendly haunters. In most cases, they are unaware how they affect the living. They do not know or understand that they are dead. We, the living, are in their space and may even appear as ghosts to them! When encountering such energies, we need to bear in mind that these are "lost souls" who are earthbound, having not yet found their way to the light. (See Chapter 2, Spiritual Hierarchy.)

In an early documented record of a haunting in a house in Athens, clanking chains were heard followed by the appearance of a disheveled old man. No one would stay in the house except one man, Athenodorus, who had little money and the rent was dirt cheap. The ghost appeared on several occasions and finally led the tenant to a spot in the garden. Athenodorus began digging there and found a skeleton with chains attached. This discovery stopped the hauntings (Guiley, 1992, p. 22).

Another tale tells of a bridge in Rome called the Ponte Sisto, over the Tiber River. The story was that, on very dark nights, people sighted a black coach drawn by black horses, crossing the bridge. An old woman holding coffers of gold rode inside the carriage. This was the ghost of Olympia Maidalchini Pamphili, the mistress of Pope Innocent X. At her lover's deathbed, she stole his money and left him to die alone. The nightly jaunts across the bridge are said to be her journey into hell to pay for all her sins. In this incidence, the ghost was not bothering anyone. It was simply an earthbound spirit held on this plane by her own actions (Time-Life, 1984, p. 95).

The British Isles, the source of numerous stories of castle hauntings, has one particular story about Castle Glamis in

Scotland. This castle boasts several phantoms dating back to the fourteenth century. They let their presences be known by unearthly noises and ghostly appearances in the form of monsters, skeletons, a tongueless woman and a white lady. It is believed that one of the Lords of Glamis put a curse on all his descendants that all deceased family members were destined to be earth-bound in his castle (Time-Life, 1984, pp. 86–91).

One ghost, who was finally freed from wandering and haunting, was the bride of Marwell Hall in England. Apparently, on her wedding night, the lady played a game of hide and seek so well that she could not be found. The house and surrounding areas were searched in vain. When her spirit began to haunt the manor by floating up and down stairways and rattling door locks, her groom knew his bride was dead. The body was finally discovered in the attic in an old locked trunk, and the manor was freed of haunting (Time-Life, 1984, p. 99).

An undesirable such ghost resides in the small town of Gore Bay, a picturesque town overlooking the North Channel in Northern Ontario.

The Thorburn House, built in 1881, has had two owners, the first being the Thorburn family. The Cook/McQuarrie family has resided there for the last 65 odd years. Over the years I have spent many nights in this house. There was never a night I was not awakened by strange, eerie noises and a heavy pressure on my chest. As a child, these activities frightened me so much that I would lie in bed with the covers pulled over my head. Yet, my aunt lived there undisturbed and unafraid. She use to joke that "Old lady Thorburn was walking around," to explain the noises. It was only in my later years that I heard the tragic story of this family.

Around the turn of the century, Mr. Thorburn took his five-year-old son on a fishing tug. The child fell overboard and drowned. As was the custom before the advent of funeral parlors, his body was brought ashore and laid out in the living room. The boy's spirit was trapped in this house because he died a tragic death.

Sixty years ago a neighbor who was in a very agitated state came over to my aunt's house. He was experiencing marital problems and wanted to talk to someone. Because he was so distraught, my aunt persuaded him to sleep over. The guestroom was the same as the little boy's who had drowned. While everyone was asleep, the man left and drowned himself in the bay, in front of the house.

Recently my sister visited this house with her dog. The dog exhibited peculiar behavior, staying very close to my sister. It is usually a very rambunctious animal, always exploring places where it shouldn't. The dog spotted something on the staircase and left my sister's side. It twisted its head in apparent disbelief and returned shaking and growling to the protection of her mistress. My sister did not see anything but did sense an unnatural presence.

THE UGLY

Just as there are good and bad people on this earth, there are good and bad entities. Evil spirits are better known as **poltergeists**, the translation from German meaning "noisy spirit." They can be a collection of negative energies and thought forms from a group of spirits, or **astral garbage**—a conglomeration of destructive energies. The mixture is so volatile that it explodes in this dimension, manifesting as lifting, rearranging, moving, throwing and destroying objects. Whatever the source, there is no doubt about anyone sensing the presence of poltergeists. Whether you are a kinesethic, auditory or visual perceiver, this type of energy manifests with a vengeance. When we are in contact with such a force field, it is as if we are tangled in a sticky web of energy.

Poltergeists are readily distinguishable from ghosts. They can cause object movement, disappearance and destruction. This type of energy can actually attack and harm us. It typically chooses a person to vent its evil on rather than a place, even following this unlucky soul from place to place. On the other hand, ghosts do not harm or attack people, preferring to stay at their regular haunts.

An extreme case of such an attack was made famous by William Peter Blatty's *The Exorcist*. The original story involved a young boy. When he reached the age of thirteen, in 1949, strange phenomena began occurring in the family's house in Washington D.C. Signs of intruding energies were scratching noises, movement of objects, the boy's bed shaking, removal of his sheets, marks on his skin and the coughing of phlegm. All of these misdemeanors were attributed to poltergeist activities (Guiley, 1992, p. 226).

In the past, it was believed children were unwilling assistants to poltergeist. Invasions were attributed to hormonal changes occurring around puberty. These destructive energies would be attracted to a person with a soft, malleable aura.

As a child develops and matures, s/he moves away from the natural protective aura of her/his parents. The child takes on her/his own identity and set of energies more strongly at the age of puberty. At this time of severing ties with Mom and Dad, children are fairly vulnerable and are therefore more susceptible to attack.

Poltergeist activity can also manifest in specific places. If the conditions are right, they will be there, as was the case of Lois and Harvey's house. Not only does this couple encounter ghosts, but poltergeist intruders as well dwelled in their home. The strange set of circumstances present for this type of materialization were:

1. *The house was built near a body of water and had several underground streams criss-crossing the property.*
2. *There already were two ghosts (Jake and the gardener) on the property.*
3. *Lois's mother had been unhappy in the house (releasing her negativity into the structure).*
4. *The house had numerous people living there over the years before Lois and Harvey moved in as a couple.*
5. *There was an incompatible energy fusion from artifacts gathered from all over the globe.*
6. *Harvey's mother was psychically attacking her son.*

All of these separate occurrences and energies mixed together to create a nightmare. According to Lois, the house rebelled against them. Pipes froze, doors mysteriously locked, renovations were sabotaged. Discord prevailed. A final incident that caused the couple to seek the services of a professional entity remover occurred when Lois was struck by the poltergeist energy. Seconds before the attack, the air turned a bone chilling cold and gray mist seemed to swirl about the room. The energies were gathering in strength, momentum and destruction. Lois was hit on the arm and then later on her back before she and her husband could leave the house. A psychic finally removed this conglomeration of negative energy. The couple now lives in harmony within the walls of this house minus the poltergeist energy.

As Sheila Hervey said in her book, *Canada Ghost to Ghost,* "A poltergeist is simply a nightmare come true." (For further details of the Lois and Harvey's nightmare occurrence refer to this book).

PSYCHIC ATTACK

A person can be under psychic attack from discarnate beings or a powerful person(s). Psychic attacks can also come in the forms of **curses, hexes, the Evil Eye, and revenge.**

The signs of entity attack are very definitive. This intrusion can occur between wakefulness and sleep when consciousness is just beginning to slip. As explained in Chapter 4, The Veil Is Lifted, this is when spontaneous out-of-body experiences happen. There is the sensation of pressure on the chest area ranging from just a slight sense of weight to the feeling that someone is actually sitting on you. Then your body will also begin to feel weightless, as if it were slipping away from conscious control.

My personal experience with an O.B.E. began with a crushing heaviness over my heart. I immediately panicked, which increased the sensation. I opened my eyes to see a grayish vapor hovering over my body. I had also experienced a different kind of attack from unseen forces several years ago when I first opened up my psychic awareness. I would be awakened during the night to the sensation of having my bedclothes pulled off while sensing unusual energies surrounding me. Since I was more asleep than awake, I felt little or no control over my body. I was stroked and caressed by these energies and then would fall into a deep sleep. Because I believed these were a loving group of entities, I was not too alarmed. This pattern was repeated over the next several weeks. While attending a seminar given by Dr. Frank Alper, Adamis Enterprises, I had more intense experiences. This time the beings appeared to me. The following morning I asked Frank if he could ascertain what was going on. He immediately alerted me to the fact that I was under psychic attack and subsequently removed these energies. Yet, I pondered over this occurrence for many years until the reason for the attack finally dawned on me. I had opened myself up too quickly, without the proper protection. Once again, I learned my lesson, the hard way.

Dion Fortune, in *Psychic Self-Defense*, writes that in addition to the crushing weight on the chest, more symptoms of psychic attack can be unexplained bruises or injuries to the body.

A group or person who has in-depth occult expertise can also perpetuate psychic attack. Such persons can be gurus, teachers or Wicca masters. If this type of person wishes to dominate others with a similar degree of awareness, then the victims easily fall prey to attack. There are many false teachers who wish to control and manipulate their followers. Throughout history, people have sacrificed their individuality and rights for what they believed to be a leader's higher ideals. Using mind control many cult leaders have persuaded followers to perform acts of suicide in the name of their cause. In November of 1978, over nine hundred members of a cult, led by Jim Jones, committed mass suicide by drinking cyanide. They believed Armageddon was imminent. In April of 1993, the Branch Davidian in Waco Texas suffered thirty-three deaths, many of which were children. March 26, 1997 saw thirty-nine members of Heaven's Gate commit mass suicide. These people believed the appearance of the comet Hale-Bopp was the sign they had been waiting for: their spacecraft had arrived to take cult members home.

These three tragedies were all the result of members influenced by very powerful leaders. Some definite signs that you are under the influence of a powerful person's attack are continuous obsessive thoughts about them, dreaming of situations where they are involved, deterioration of your relationship with family, friends and partners, loss of physical strength and energy, and uncharacteristic mood changes. My own experiences with this form of psychic attack originated from a powerful person who was very experienced in the occult. For some reason, he felt the need to draw me into his energies. His name kept popping into my mind; I sensed his heaviness around me day and night. I was at odds with my family over little matters that never used to bother me. After days of suffering with this intrusion, I realized what was happening. Through aura strengthening exercises, I was able to remove my energies from this person's psychic influences.

Curses are a form of psychic attack directed by humans against places, objects or people. An ancient North American aboriginal curse is the Bearwalk, a negative thought form directed at a person giving them "bad medicine" or difficulties in life. Symbolically the bear, a token of powerful fear, walks over the aura of the victim. The symptoms of such an attack include the victim imagining frightening images, having reoccurring nightmares, experiencing sickness or in extreme cases death, alcoholism and mental instability.

Samples of curses associated to places are Egyptian tombs, infamous for dire results to intruders. Thought forms were placed around the objects of the deceased. If anyone disturbed these burial areas, they would be damned. There are several documented cases, such as Lord Carnarvon, who opened Tutankhamun's tomb, later dying of an infected mosquito bite. Others associated with his archeological party also died under strange circumstances. Whether the deaths were from noxious gases or a curse, the thought form of revenge was embedded in the tomb.

Modern day **hexes** can have power over their victims. A friend in Egypt suddenly experienced anxiety attacks for no apparent reason. She became very distraught when some crudely made cloth dolls with pins were found hidden in various spots of her garden. Although no physical pain was suffered, my friend was very emotionally upset. It was later discovered the attacker was a servant recently dismissed who was seeking revenge on her mistress by trying this ancient hex.

The **Evil Eye** is another form of psychic intrusion. Modern western culture has very little idea of its power. The idiom "If looks could kill" refers to a belief the eye can harm or hurt others by its expression. In ancient times, the evil eye was blamed for death, disease and disaster. In the Middle East great precautions are taken to repel its assault. For example, if a woman was looking at another's baby, instead of admiring the child she would say, "What an ugly baby." This is suppose to ward off the evil eye, which is envy. If the beauty of the child had been commented on, the belief is held that the baby would be subjected to sickness or another type of negative energy. When my son was born in this part of the world, it took a lot of mental rethinking when others told me how ugly he was!

The final form of psychic attack, which is deliberately unleashed by someone, is **revenge**. An angered person can generate a massive negative force field, affecting both the perpetrator and the victim. Symptoms are chakra bleeding, usually at the base center. It is an astral or etheric leaking in which the victim senses the life force being drained out of her/her.

This type of vengeful psychic attack was unleashed on me by a woman who believed that I had taken away her husband. In actual fact, I met him after his separation but she needed someone to vent her anger towards. Whenever she thought of us, I could feel a leaking of energy from my base chakra. Often, within minutes of this sensation beginning, there would be a telephone call. She would be on the line ranting and raving, spewing her venom. I always felt like a wet dishrag after each attack. It was only after learning to seal my aura that this form of psychic attack ceased.

ASTRAL DEBRIS

Astral debris or garbage is energy that is left over from living persons. It does not necessarily refer to negative vibrations but is unwanted, serving no purpose. Through being in a location with a group of people, our aura absorbs their collective mental and emotional states. This garbage can then be carried about in our auras, affecting our well being and causing disturbances in our dream state. Before learning to close my aura, I would constantly dream about the children that I had been teaching that day. I always woke up exhausted. I was sponging up all their unexpressed thoughts and desires. I was getting stuck on the astral plane and was being robbed of a deep, rejuvenating sleep.

We can soak up astral debris from events as well. As a teenager, I would attend local teen dances. The music was blaring. Young people's emotional, mental and hormonal energies were flying around the room. Later, when sleeping, I invariably dreamt I was still at the dance. I would see the teenagers and hear the music. I absorbed all the psychic energy from the people, sounds and place.

It is common occurrence for friends to share their problems. Being in the presence of a special friend who unburdens her soul to you can be detrimental if your aura is not properly protected. Dreaming about this person, or carrying her problems as your own, means your aura is too open. Their negative energy and thought patterns have impregnated us.

People will carry the above types of astral debris with them for a few minutes, days or longer depending on how open their auras are. It naturally evaporates over a period of time, perhaps days or weeks. Until this debris leaves, the host is affected. Depression and irritability are common side effects. In extreme cases, a person may become sick with flu-like symptoms. This is a purging/cleansing by the body to rid negative energies. And, it is very difficult in most incidents to determine whether this is astral garbage or our own trash. Whatever the source, we need to get rid of it!

Astral garbage can also be picked up through ingesting foods prepared by persons who are releasing negative energies. If we stop and think about restaurant food, we have no idea whose or the kind of vibrations are permeating our meals. If the food preparer is going through a negative period, i.e. animosity towards his boss, then his entire aura will radiate these vibrations which are naturally transferred to the food. If we are the least bit sensitive, we will pick up these unhealthy energies and have physical reactions like stomach cramping, indigestion, diarrhea or headache. We indeed do have a case of food poisoning!

A further type of astral debris can literally weigh us down. While I was leisurely strolling in a nearby park, contemplating the writing of this book, my attention was drawn to a man who was jogging. The sun was hidden behind clouds, making perfect conditions for aura gazing. There seemed to be a parcel of energy attached to this man. It was as if a heavy sack was tied onto his upper back. It radiated at least 5 feet from him. From what I could determine, he probably felt he had the whole weight of the world on him, and astrally it was! The poor fellow was carrying unwanted baggage.

HUMAN PARASITES

The next type of intruding forces are the energies emitted by the human parasites. These are the people who attach themselves to others at a subconscious level. (See Chapter 5). The signs that our energies have been invaded are feeling a pulling or tightening on our power center, the solar plexus, fatigue, depression and the overall feeling of being drained.

A relative has this type of affect on my family. The minute he enters our home, I protect it with a white light to dispel his negative nature. He incessantly talks about himself and his accomplishments. He never listens to others, just using us as an audience. We do not have the heart to turn him away, as we realize he is in need of deep love and nurturing. Inadvertently, I would cross my arms over my solar plexus to prevent astral leakage and his etheric attachment to my energies. This type of parasite is preying on others' loving and understanding natures. We need to protect ourselves from such invading energies. We no longer have to be the victims of negativity!

KARMIC SPIRITS

The final type of energy invasion is from beings that have karmic attachments to us. A karmic spirit possession or attachment can be difficult to uncover. A spirit can follow us from one lifetime to another. This apparition may be someone from several past incarnations, to whom we have caused harm or who was deeply connected to us through a love or family situation. Whatever the reason, there is a strong attachment. Our souls have made an agreement to have the entity attach itself to us. There is some negative or positive karma between us. This being is anchored in the astral plane, not able to move on to the light until the debt has been cancelled. Each time we reincarnate, it influences our energies. While we are up in the higher dimensions, between lives, it may or may not be able to reach us, depending on its level of consciousness. But, while we are on the lower plane of earth, it can effect us in either a positive or negative way.

Kevin Fitzpatrick of St. George Ontario is a renowned psychic reader. While I was interviewing him for this book, he told me that I had an old war spirit attached to me. He had been with me for the past two lifetimes. I had no idea this being was sharing my energies. The only inclination I had a presence, not of my own, was when I would pass a Red Cross Blood Clinic, chills would creep all over my body. When I closed my eyes, I could see battles, from what appeared to be the last two world wars. Since I was not carnate for either of these wars, in this lifetime or past, I knew the Red Cross' symbol was significant for him. He must have witnessed these wars while on the astral plane and was projecting their horrors to me. Through past life regression, I learned that this being was related to me. He was indebted to me for helping him in a past situation. He was subsequently sent to the light and I no longer have his energies around me. His debt and mine were completed.

For researching this type of being, if there is not a satisfactory completion between the spirit and ourselves, then the attachment will continue until whatever past life issues there existed have been resolved. (See Chapter 8.)

CONCLUSION

We must demonstrate responsibility and not assume that every time we feel depressed or overly tired, that an attack is happening. A drop in physical energy, for no apparent reason (i.e. you are not coming down with a virus, not overworked or stressed) is not cause for alarm. Some questions to ask yourself before assuming you are being invaded are:

1) Were other people around me at the time I felt the sensation? In other words, was I subjected to a thought form or some type of psychic attack?

2) Was I in an area where there could have been negative energies? (a bar, hospital, etc.)

3) Was I around people who were negative in nature? (i.e. human parasites)

4) What cycle am I in (female), re hormonal changes? (explains personality alterations)

5) What prescription drugs am I currently taking? Are my mind, body, perception and/or mood, being altered due to a medication?

Keep a diary and record any new sensations or occurrences and then decide if you are experiencing an invasion.

There are numerous forces surrounding us. These can be in the form of possessions, ghosts, poltergeists, psychic attacks, human parasites, astral garbage and karmic attachments. Having established awareness of forces, their sources and influences, we can move on to methods for their removal, so we can fully live and work in the light.

Be at peace and
See a clear
Pattern running
Through all your lives.
Nothing is by chance.

Eileen Cady, *Footprints on the Path*

CHAPTER SEVEN

New Age Remedies for Age Old Problems

IN THE PREVIOUS CHAPTER, various kinds of energy intrusions were exposed. These invaders have been around since the dawn of civilization. Our forefathers, using materials at hand, devised various methods to ward off evil spirits. Making the sign of a cross over the chest, or wearing one of silver was considered a protection against ghosts and evil entities. Garlic was used to ward off vampire attacks. Fingers were crossed to keep witches away. Sprinkling Holy Water on houses and people chased out the devil. Salt was strewn across thresholds to protect against malicious spirits. A horseshoe nailed over the front door was used as a charm to bring good fortune to the household. Talismans made from pentagrams and other shapes kept demons at bay. Amulets with precious stones protected wearers from negative vibrations. One such Biblical reference (Exodus 28) was Aaron who received divine orders to construct a breastplate with twelve precious gemstones. Each jewel represented a tribe of Israel. Over his heart were the Urim and Thummin stones. One, believed to be smoky quartz, and the other, clear, were to protect Aaron in his battle against evil forces.

Today, the significance of protecting and warding off evil is still a genuine concern. It follows suite, that in this new age, we can adapt and incorporate the wisdom of the ancients. Those simple and effective old age remedies, combined with our new age knowledge, can render us impervious to negativity.

The following chapter is divided into three sections. Each form of negative, intruding energy is addressed. In the first section, guidance is given for modifying internal thinking patterns and fortifying the aura. The second deals with ways to expel human parasites and astral debris. The final section addresses the removal of ghosts and poltergeists. It is the task of the reader to earnestly work on one's self to remove all traces of negativity. A summary of remedies related to their corresponding intruders is given as a quick reference at the end of this chapter.

SECTION ONE
THOUGHT FORMS AND FORTIFYING THE AURA

In earlier chapters, the fragility of the aura was alluded to. We have learned why unwanted entities and energies can prey on and invade us. Therefore it is of utmost importance to take the necessary precautions to protect the aura.

The aura houses our physical, etheric, emotional, mental and spiritual energies. It has a big job protecting its inner energies, while fending off external vibrations. We need to keep in mind the kind of internal activity, within the confines of the aura that directly affects its resistance capabilities. By reversing any destructive thoughts, our vibrations will be raised above the astral plane so the lower entities and thought forms will no longer affect us.

Affirmations, flower remedies, gem elixirs, crystals, aura strengthening exercises, gemstone wearing, symbols, and essences are just a few means for altering thought forms and strengthening the aura.

The first aura treatment is to eliminate any negative, undesirable and self-defeating thoughts. Chapter 2 on "Thought Forms" emphasized our vulnerability to all thought vibrations. Loving, detrimental, creative, depressive, healthy, diseased and destructive thoughts float around the outer shell of our auras. It is up to us to select which ones we allow through into our personal energy fields. Only by examining, then clearing, any undesirable conscious and subconscious thoughts can we attract the Universal Frequencies of Ascension. Unconditional love, inspiration, guidance, creativity, connections with Masters and Angels, and abundance are all available for us to tap into.

We can reach into these higher vibrations of light by altering our thought patterns. The subconscious requires new messages. Any detrimental, self-defeating thoughts need to be released. This transformation of the subconscious allows the conscious to follow suit.

There are many ways to begin inner reprogramming. One method is to repeat **affirmations,** whenever a destructive thought surfaces. Since thoughts manifest quickly, a negative one must be immediately counteracted with a positive. For example, if you entertain the thought, "I got wet in the rain, so now I will get sick," instantly say, "I am strong and healthy. Sickness has no place in my life."

The positive cancels out the energy of the negative. Or, if feeling incapable of completing a project, say out loud, because sound increases the intensity of the vibration and brings it into the third dimension, "I am able to complete this project in love and harmony. I have the talents and guidance to make it the best I am capable of." The actual words do not matter. It is the thought generated that has the power.

Affirmations are just the beginning of a self-cleanse. There are many new age remedies to assist in releasing locked in negativity. **Flower remedies** are effective in ridding the subconscious of negative programming. White chestnut, vervain and willow release suppressed anger from our subtle bodies. Aspen liberates fear. Certo works on increasing self-confidence. **Gem elixirs** have similar healing properties. Fluorite assists in releasing sexual conflicts, ruby works on loosening up rigid thinking, and lapis enhances self-expression.

Crystal and gem healing layouts remove undesirable energies from the aura. There are many arrangements given in this author's *Crystal Awareness* and *Crystal Ascension* books.

Holistic health practitioners are available to assist with thought and energy transformations. Radionics, touch for health, Reiki, massage, regression, rebirthing and many other methods are offered. There are many self-help books, seminars, groups and teachers who provide guidance and direction in getting in touch with our inner self. There are so many possibilities that there no longer is any valid excuse for us not working at releasing undesirable thoughts.

With the raising of our consciousness, the further we are able to delve into our spirituality. Simultaneously, our aura expands, reflecting the changing brilliance of our Inner Light. And, it becomes stronger and more discerning. It begins to cleanse itself whenever negativity is encountered without our conscious effort. However, we need to set the conditions for this to automatically manifest and, until it does, it is advisable to invoke the following two strengthening exercises using white light and a violet vortex.

White Light

Invoking a cleansing, white light is an ageless method to protect self from all types of energy intrusions of both human and spirit form. This simple process may be performed before entering a negative place such as a hospital or group of people who drain your energy. It can be invoked if a possession or ghost is present.

White, the blending of all color is used for a total cleansing and purification. This is accomplished by mentally imagining every single cell in your body as vibrating white light (refer to diagram).

STEP ONE
- Close your eyes and take a deep breath.
- See each cell radiating like a tiny flame of light. The flame starts on the surface of the skin and radiates out one inch.
- Envision these lights expanding and glowing stronger and further out from your skin.
- See your etheric body illuminated in white light.

STEP TWO
- Expand the light to encompass the emotional and mental bodies.
- The light is now radiating 6 feet in all directions from your skin.
- Direct it further to fill your entire aura.

STEP THREE
- Expand it out further and further until you can no longer "see" it with your inner vision. You have become the light. You and the light are one.

STEP FOUR
- Clap your hands or snap your fingers to complete and affirm that what has been done in the spiritual plane manifests in the third dimension.
- Repeat this exercise as often as needed. Tell yourself to have the light automatically activated whenever negativity comes into your being.

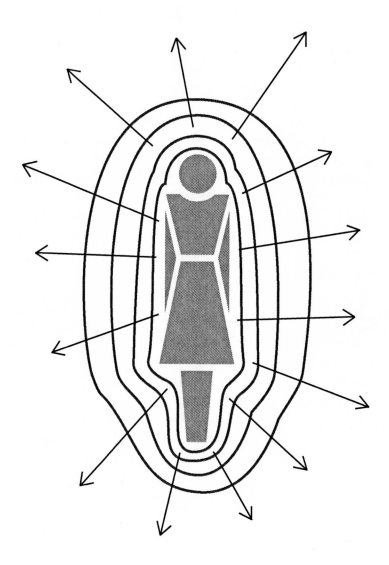

Violet Vortex

A further cleansing technique can be created with a violet hue. Violet is an effective cleansing and spiritual color. It is used to clear heavy energy and then transmute this same negativity into a higher vibration. Not only are undesirable energies transcended but the source is cleared as well. Like the White Light, it can be used on all types of entity and human intrusion. It is especially effective to self-cleanse undesirable thoughts such as anger, hatred and envy. Depending on the intensity of the thought generated, it may or may not be easily cleared before permanent damage occurs. For example when you get really mad, a red-hot searing emotion that boils from within, this emotion can be released through angry words. When this occurs, not only do you need to cleanse yourself but also the thought form that has been projected into the atmosphere. The cause and effect must be cleared. This is done by:

STEP ONE
- Close your eyes. Take a deep breath. Slowly exhale. Take another and slowly release.
- Imagine a circular, purple disk about the size of a hoola hoop forming above the top of your head. See it hovering over the crown chakra like a mini tornado of swirling purple mist.

STEP TWO
- Begin to shape the vortex into a spiral of light with the funnel directed at your crown.
- Rotate it in a clockwise direction as it gathers speed and momentum.

STEP THREE
- Have this purple vortex enter your crown and swirl through the very center of your being. As it passes down through your center, ensure that it also encompasses the outer area of the physical body. The projected energy field should surround your entire being.

STEP FOUR
- Once the vortex reaches your feet, envision it entering the ground, going down a further three feet below you.
- At this point, have the vortex reverse its flow to counter-clockwise, to re-enter your body, rising from the feet through the center of your being, up to the crown.

STEP FIVE
- When the energy reaches the crown, release it into the atmosphere. This is best done by visualizing the energy as a purple mist blown away from the earth.
- This exercise can be repeated if you are still feeling any heavy unwanted energies around you.

The Purple Vortex may be performed several times a day, whenever you feel the need to release unwanted emotions, attitudes or thoughts.

AURA ENHANCERS

There are many types of aura enhancing devices that we borrowed from our forefathers. Some are the use of **gemstones and crystals, symbols, flower extracts and vibrational enhancers.**

Crystal/Gemstone Wearing

Precious stones and crystals can be used to protect our auras. Both minerals have been employed for this purpose throughout the ages. Ancient talismans and amulets containing stones and quartz crystals were indigenous in Egyptian, Roman, Greek, Chinese, Incan and North American Indian cultures. Turquoise, lapis lazuli, jade, ruby and quartz brought magical powers and protection to wearers. If the individual believed in the power of the talisman, that conviction would generate the thought of protection.

Today, some people wear stones as jewelry for personal adornment, unaware of the subconscious reasons. Consciously wearing a natural quartz crystal pendant, so it rests over the heart chakra, sets up powerful energy fields. Not only does the crystal continuously cleanse the aura, but it also links the wearer to higher dimensions. It transcends negative vibrations that may emanate from entities and humans. After paying a visit to a place which had the potential of being a source of considerable negativity, such as a doctor's office, courtroom, police station or bar, it is advisable to soak the pendant in a solution of salt and water (½ cup to 1 quart of water) for at least four hours. Rinse in cool, clear running water and resume wearing. Gemstones can be used in the same manner although their power is not as profound as the natural quartz. (For further information see this author's books, *Crystal Awareness* and *Crystal Ascension*.)

Symbols

A very powerful method of protecting self against any kind of invading energy, from human thought forms or spirits, is by using a personal symbol. Symbols are spiritual reminders, encouraging and guiding us throughout our lives.

Everyone responds to a different symbol, one that has an uniquely, powerful meaning. It may be in the ordinary shape of a flower, a complicated mathematical configuration, or have esoteric significance as in the pentagram, cross or Star of David, or like no other symbol on earth.

Your symbol can appear through a dream or meditative state. Or, you may be drawn to a particular object or picture. The concept of having a symbol as a type of talisman was so simple that I long ignored it. Years ago, I created an Atlantian symbol as a logo for my business cards. There it was, patiently staring at me, unused all of those years. When I began to utilize this particular shape for protection, I immediately felt positive effects.

It does not matter what the symbol is or how it is found. Whatever the source, you will know when you discover it by the way your entire being resonates with its protective powers. Investigate and determine what your special sign is. Be assured it has been waiting for you!

Once your unique symbol is established, the next step is to use it to fortify the aura. This is done by projecting the symbol into your energy field whenever you are about to enter an uncomfortable place or situation. Start visualizing this sign, in whatever size you wish, as being centered over your heart chakra. Next, imagine it growing and expanding, until the symbol completely surrounds your being. Then, expand it further until it fills your entire aura. Your physical and spiritual self will be protected. You have created a personal, powerful talisman.

I was recently involved in helping remove negative energies from a house in my neighborhood. Before entering the home, I fortified my aura with White Light and the Purple Vortex. I still felt vulnerable until I added my personal symbol. Then, I "knew" I was protected at all levels.

Essences

A variety of old age remedies (under new age labels) which strengthen the aura are on the market. These flower and homeopathic essences work on the subtle bodies over a period of time. A few of the ingredients are snapdragon, tansy, yarrow and shooting star. They build an energy shield around the aura, increasing its repelling capabilities. Homeopathic drugs can also be used to perform the same defensive actions.

Vibrational Enhancers

There are many products available to enhance, restore, harmonize and align the aura. One such device is an imprinted card which, when worn either around the neck or carried in a pocket, will continuously repel any negative thought forms or astral debris. Another is a small quartz crystal pendant, which strengthens the aura and transcends any type of destructive energy. These methods are carefree, because the wearer does not have to perform any conscious effort, just wear the amulet.

SECTION TWO

This section deals with third-dimensional negativity generated by humans, astral debris and possessions. The new age cures for age old problems are **creating a wall, love energy, water, salt, incense, candles, music, hand clapping, crystals, sand, sulfur** and **hands-on removal techniques**.

When in the presence of negative people, **create a wall** between you and that person or persons. Image a solid brick wall about seven feet tall in front of you so it blocks their energies from reaching yours. It only takes a second to erect a strong wall. (You may to wish to imagine mirrors on their side of the wall to reflect their negativity back to them.)

If someone is verbally abusive, a very effective way to protect yourself and help the abuser is to transmit **love energy**. To do this, close your eyes and visualize a bright pink ray of color surrounding this person. A violet-green color ray may also be used. All of these hues radiate unconditional love and healing which is really what the person is lacking.

After being in the presence of a person who tried to overwhelm you by being a human parasite or psychically attacking you, a **self cleanse** is recommended. Water has always been a vehicle for purification. It is the symbol of spiritual cleansing. Bathing in or pouring it refreshes the body, removing impurities caught in the aura. **Holy water** is used in baptisms and to bless. This water actually originated from sacred wells, having natural mineral contents. The Church uses Holy Water to ward off the devil/evil spirits. Because of its purifying energies, entities cannot come near a person or place that has been sprinkled with this water.

Salt can be combined with water to ensure a thorough cleansing. Adding a cup of natural sea salt granules to a bath does wonders to soothe and refresh.

HUMAN PARASITES
AND PSYCHIC ATTACHMENTS

Removing another person's aka thread attachment can be accomplished by a partner or your own efforts. This type of energy connection can manifest from a former lover we are unable to disassociate from. We cannot stop thinking about this person. It does not matter if the overriding emotion is anger, remorse, guilt or love. His/her energies are still with us. On the opposite side, we could be completely over this person, but s/he is still attached to us. Either way, the energy needs to be cleared.

Astral bleeding was mentioned earlier. This psychic energy drain due to a person's all-consuming anger towards us has to be resolved, or we are in danger of getting mentally, emotionally or physically ill.

An abusive partner can be psychically attacking us even if we are removed from his or her presence. The aka threads are still linked to our chakras and need severing so each party can get on with their lives.

Partner Assistance

For partner-assisted removal of the energies from a human parasite or psychic attack, the same serene, comfortable environment as with the possession removals will need to be created. You also require seven natural quartz crystals, one being a larger size with an intact termination, the others, smaller single points. The generator or larger quartz can vary in size from 3 to 7 inches.

Have a blanket nearby, in case your partner feels cold. You need to invoke White Light or the Violet Vortex, as well as asking for the assistance of your guides and those of your partner's.

STEP ONE
- Have your partner lie face up, on a comfortable surface.
- Soft music will enhance this person drifting into a peaceful meditative state.

STEP TWO
- Take the larger crystal in the hand where it feels most comfortable. Hold it point down over the crown chakra of your partner, about 4 inches away from the body (see diagram).

- You will be slicing through the etheric webbing, which radiates 4 to 6 inches beyond the physical body. You will not touch your partner's third-dimensional body.

Point

Largest facet

STEP THREE

- Run the crystal's apex (point) down the center of your partner, passing over the third eye, throat, heart, solar plexus, spleen and base chakras. Continue down between the legs to the feet, as if you were drawing a line to divide the body in half.

STEP FOUR

- Once the etheric cut has been made, you have an entrance to the physical body.

STEP FIVE

- With the large crystal, test each chakra of your partner for energy imbalances (method used by Dr. Frank Alper of Adamis Enterprises).
- Take your large crystal; gently touch the point to your partner's body where the base chakra is. Ask your partner, while you are touching the crystal over this area, to respond with the first thing that comes to mind. A response might be, "I see red," indicating the chakra is open and clear of intrusions. Others could be "I hurt"; "I feel cold, happy, sad or absolutely nothing." These are indicative of aka attachments. Even if s/he feels nothing, you need to know this. If you get a positive response, such as the chakra's color or a joyful answer, the chakra is open and functioning well. If the partner feels nothing or

you get a negative response, gently rotate the tip of your crystal clockwise for a few turns directly on his/her body. This action will release any energy intrusions and build up of undesirable vibrations. Depending on your intuitiveness and comfort level, you may pick up the response before your partner actually verbalizes it. You may "see" the attachment to another person or "feel" the intrusion.

• Gently place one of the seven smaller crystals point up towards the head over this center, even if no negativity was felt. A balancing is still needed.

STEP SIX
• Repeat the above process over the spleen chakra and the rest of the centers.
• At the crown center, rest this area's crystal against the head at the hairline, point up.

STEP SEVEN
• Keep the crystals on the person's body for at least 10 minutes. Cover your partner with a blanket, and allow her/him to rest undisturbed.

STEP EIGHT
• Gently remove the blanket and each crystal.

STEP NINE
• With your large crystal, retest each chakra by asking the same questions, while touching each center. If a negative response is still given, you and your partner need to decide whether or not to repeat this crystal placement, now, or at a later time. There may be more than one energy attachment and more treatment needed.
• If the session is over, hold your healing crystal with its base touching your palm. Your thumb and pointer finger

will cover the apex (point), leaving one facet open to the air, preferably the largest one (see diagram).

- Holding this position, generate a beam of light (white or purple) in your solar plexus center. Imagine it travelling up through your body and out the arm holding the crystal. That beam is going to project, like a laser, out the largest facet exposed in your palm.

STEP TEN

- Stand over your partner and hold the crystal about 6 inches from his/her body. Beam that ray of light, through the crystal, at each of your partner's chakras, starting at the base and working your way up to the crown.

STEP ELEVEN

- Gently close the aura by swirling the crystal on its side, still in the same position in the hand, over the entire body.

STEP TWELVE

- Hold your crystal so the point is exposed.
- Touch the skin of your partner's forehead on the third eye with its crystal point.
- You have further sealed the aura.

Self-Energy Removal

A variation of the above can be done when treating yourself. You will need all seven crystals close by, for easy access.

STEP ONE

- Lie face up on a comfortable surface.
- Invoke the white light and ask for spirit teachers and guides to assist you.

STEP TWO
- Take the larger crystal and divide your aura, from the crown to your base.

STEP THREE
- Touch the crystal directly on your body at the base chakra.
- Note the kind of response you get. You may see a color, hear a sound, or receive an impression. Perhaps you will sense coldness, warmth, tingling or nothing. As with the partner method, any positive sensation indicates no energy attachment. Any coldness, nothingness, negative emotional or mental response means the area is vulnerable.
- Gently rotate the crystal's point over the base in a clockwise direction for a few turns.
- Lay one of the smaller, single crystal's point up on this center.

STEP THREE
- Repeat this process for the remaining six centers.

STEP FOUR
- Lie still with all the crystals on your chakras for at least 10 minutes.
- Drift into a meditate state and allow your thoughts to come and go at will.

STEP FIVE
- Remove each quartz and retest yourself by touching each center with your large crystal. If negativity or attachment is still experienced over any center, repeat the process at another session.

STEP SIX
- Hold the larger crystal in your palm as in the previous PARTNER instructions.
- Close your aura by touching your third eye with the crystal point.

STEP SEVEN
- You may rise or stay in this position and perform the aura strengthening meditation given at the back of this book.

Some further suggestions for defending ourselves from human parasites and psychic attack are **body crossing, third eye staring, crystal clusters and spraying salt water.**

Body Crossing

When in the presence of people who zap our energy, the loss can be stopped by body crossing. Simply lace the fingers together, then place your entwined hands directly over the solar plexus area with palms facing inward. This prevents the other person's aka threads from attaching to you. Crossing the feet at the ankles will also build a closed energy source that nothing can enter.

Evil Eye Protection

The evil eye was referred to in Chapter 6. Ancient Egyptians used the Eye of Horus in tomb hieroglyphics to watch over the spirit of the dead. In the Middle East passages of the Koran are often written on the outside walls of houses in rural communities to protect the occupants. In other countries, eyes are painted on fishing boats, airplanes and other modes of transportation to keep jealous, envious thoughts at bay. Indians and Mexicans often depict the Eye of God in wall hangings to protect against these destructive emotions.

We can evoke the wisdom of our forefathers by playing religious music or reciting prayers in our homes after a negative person leaves. Or, we can counteract such negativity at the time, by intently staring at the third eye of such a person. Unwanted thoughts or attempts to control our minds will be eliminated.

Crystal Clusters

A natural quartz cluster can be placed in each room of the house to clear the energy of people and astral debris. Clusters are crystals that share a common base. There may be as few as two or as many as a hundred, in this type of configuration. Each point, within the cluster grouping, has its own unique energy pattern, yet all are in harmonious synchronicity. Their continuous recharging process makes them natural air purifiers. Amethyst clusters make excellent room cleansers because of their deep purple hues.

Salt Water

Spraying a room with a solution of sea salt and water is quick, refreshing cleanser for removal of astral garbage and others' negative thoughts. Keep a mixture at hand in a spray bottle of ½ cup of sea salt in a quart of distilled water. Our aura can also be sprayed with this solution to remove any build up of electromagnetic energies and potentially destructive vibrations.

ASTRAL DEBRIS

Each of us releases thoughts into our homes. We are accustomed to our own energies and those of our family. Allowances are made and defense mechanisms are in place to deal with the astral debris surrounding loved ones. The arrival of other energies such as overnight guests can cause havoc to existing vibrations in our home.

Being a sensitive, I use to pick up any negative or incompatible energy from people who spent time in my home, i.e., overnight. I would be irritable and depressed often for days after they left. In later years, my child reacted as I had. After realizing my family was absorbing this astral garbage, I cleansed the house thoroughly.

If you are in a room, place or building, where negativity is sensed from either astral debris or leftover thought forms, immediately use the violet **vortex** to cleanse and dissipate this unwanted energy. By invoking this light or the white light method, the area will receive a cleansing vortex of energy. When finished projecting light, fill the area with a warm, pink loving flame.

To further assist, when changing your bedclothes or guests', visualize a purple vapor cleansing the sleeping area. A great deal of spiritual healing and releasing is done during sleep. Using this purple mist ensures that no negative residue remains to be absorbed while we are sleeping.

Burning **incense,** in its pure form, is also an effective clearing agent. Incense naturally raises the vibrations of a room in which it is burning. Frankincense has been used throughout antiquity for its purification properties. It was a gift to the Christ child from the Magi. Sandalwood and rosemary are good choices for protection. Cedar and sage are strong negative thought removers. These scents can be burned while visitors are in the house. Slightly open a window, to let the undesirable energy escape. Be careful of the perfumed sticks that have flooded the market. They only produce an odor and have no purifying powers!

Candles have always been used to cast light on darkness. They were, and still are, utilized at rituals, ceremonies and celebrations. Historically, candles were used to rebuff evil spirits during religious ceremonies. There is much folklore surrounding sputtering, dimly burning and wax dripping tapers. But, the main purpose is to use the candle's light to cleanse and rid an area of negativity. Just light one any time the presence of unwanted energies is felt.

In addition to incense, harmonious, consciousness-raising **music** may be added.

I often light incense, open a window and put on a c.d. I shut the door and in 20 minutes or less, check the energy. I know it is clear by the lighter more serene vibrations in the room. I feel free of the previous stress and strain. In extreme cases, I might have to use the white or purple light for a final clearing.

To summarize, a room or entire house can be cleansed of negative thought patterns from others or our own by:
1) Burning incense
2) Surrounding self and the room with a white light or use the purple vortex
3) Burning incense and candles
4) Playing soft, tranquil music.

You may need to do one or all of the above depending on the amount of astral debris sensed.

Hand Clapping

If you are uncertain as to whether there are negative energies, spirits or thought forms in a room, clap your hands.

The sudden noise will startle any energy and cause it to break up. People involuntarily break plates or drop objects causing a noise. Again, this sound dispels any negative vibrations.

Crystal Usage

Crystals have been part of this planet's composition since the dawn of creation. This natural mineral's energies have been used in lost, ancient and modern civilizations in the technological world. An even flow of electromagnetic vibrations freely moves through the crystalline structure of spiraling triangles, making this stone a natural energy conductor.

Crystals have a more exotic function in our New Age. By releasing their energies through body and thought contact, this beautiful gift from Nature is a perfect tool for raising our consciousness. They are used for healing, transmuting negativity, raising our spiritual vibrations and for other new age therapies. The lost art of crystal usage is once again surfacing for humankind to use in assisting inner development.

Placing a clear quartz crystal cluster in the guestroom and other heavy trafficked areas of your home will eliminate negative vibrations. Program the entire crystal to remove any negativity from the atmosphere (refer to *Crystal Awareness* for details).

Crystals can also be used around the perimeters of the home to ward off human and spiritual intruders. By placing natural quartz points, points up, in the four outermost corners of your home (basement or ground floor), your house will be protected. Lower thoughts and entities will be repelled by energies within the quartz.

If crystals are not available, an equal mixture of **salt, sulfur and sand** can be used to protect you home. Coming from the earth and being crystalline in structure, they all receive, hold and release electromagnetic forces. Jody Maas, an energy worker from Hamilton, Ontario, uses the properties of these minerals to close off any potential negative entry spots in a home.

In the summer of '97, I accompanied Jody while he was ridding a home of unwanted energies. He sprinkled this mixture in sinks, toilets, showers and bathtubs (in the drains.) He flicked these particles over electrical, cable and telephone outlets to prevent intrusion. Like the folklore of throwing salt on the threshold, Jody was ensuring that no more spirits would enter the house (more on this topic later in this chapter).

POSSESSIONS

Chapter 2 on "Spiritual Hierarchy" discussed the various levels of entities. When dealing with possessions, spirits who try and take over a body and sometimes a mind, we must remember one important fact: WE ARE MORE EVOLVED THAN THE ENTITY. It was attracted to our light. Therefore, we need to fearlessly take charge. By fearing, we further weaken our aura.

Dr. Carl Wickland (1861-1945) worked with possessed people from all walks of life. He and his medium wife made an unusual team. The doctor would use a mild electrical current on the patients to force the entity to leave the body. His wife then absorbed the spirit directly into her energies. She would be the spokesperson for that possessing entity. When the spirit was finished communicating through her, it was sent away. From Wickland's studies, he ascertained that possessing entities had led superficial earthly lives. The lower mental attitudes of pride, vanity, ambition and selfishness still held them earthbound. It was only when they had transmuted these base tendencies into love and sympathy that these beings were able to move on.

Possessions are not new phenomena. In Luke 9:49 the disciple John was concerned about a man and said to Jesus, "We saw one casting out devils in thy name."

Matthew, Mark and Luke made references to Jesus casting out unclean spirits. Luke 4:33-36 cites the incident where Jesus encountered a man in a synagogue who was possessed by a "...spirit of an unclean devil." Jesus bid the spirit release the man by saying, "Hold thy peace, and come out of him."

Ephesians 6:11-12 states, "Put on the whole armor of God, that ye may be able to stand against the wiles of the devil. For we wrestle not against flesh and blood but against principalities, against powers, against the rulers of the darkness of this world, against spiritual wickedness in high places."

Christian churches have specially trained priests and ministers who exorcise demonic spirits. "Exorcise" comes from the Greek word, "exorkizein," meaning to "free evil spirits."

This "freeing" involves a struggle between the devil and the host's soul. The clergy's technique is to remain strong and keep repeating the name of Jesus, to override the devil. Some Christians believe that special members of their church have the power of laying on of hands to cast out evil spirits.

In the Old Testament, the Jewish people saw the possessing spirit of Saul being released when David played his harp. "And it came to pass when the evil spirit from God was upon Saul, that David took a harp, and played with his hand: so Saul was refreshed, and was well, and the evil spirit departed from him" (Sam. 16:23).

In the Middle East, the zar casts out the djinn, the possessing spirit, through dance and loud music. In the Far East, the priest contacts his Gods for directions on how to banish the devil. The demon is the yin and is dispelled with the yang, in the form of swords, cock's blood and firecrackers.

Removing a possessing spirit need not be a complicated or esoteric ritual. It can be easily done using some of the old age methods in conjunction with new age rituals. Ways to test for possible possession are using a **pendulum, muscle testing and radionics.**

Pendulum Testing

Some lightworkers use pendulums to detect possessions. Pendulums are an ancient method of divination. Our forefathers used rings, coins, crosses or some other small object suspended on a thread or string to test for good and evil. Holding a crystal or metal pendulum over the body meridians and chakra centers does this. The device will swing depending on how its holder has programmed it to indicate a yes or no answer. The entire body can be easily checked out in this manner.

Muscle Testing

Other practitioners rely on kinesiology to detect entities and energy intrusions. Kinesiology is the practice of testing muscles to diagnose deficiencies. Certain muscles are linked to specific organs and areas of the body. If there is a weak spot, then vitamins or methods of strengthening are suggested.

Kevin Fitzpatrick, a lightworker in Ontario, used muscle testing on me. It was through this method that my war-time spirit was discovered. Kevin said he felt it as an irritation in my kidneys. He saw it in my aura, as a gridwork of energy hovering around me. He released the being by sending it to the light. This entity was apparently attached to my husband as well. Both of us had incurred a karmic relationship with this being. We are now cleared of it.

Radionics

In the late 19th century, Dr. Albert Abrams developed a diagnostic tool that determined the underlying cause of disease. Today, drops of blood or hair samples are analyzed by radionics machines, and then the disease is treated with varying electronic frequencies. Some practitioners use the "black box" to remove negative thought patterns and entity attachments from clients. This controversial field of treatment is usually combined with homeopathy and other new-age treatments.

POSSESSION REMOVAL

Spirits can be removed by a partner or by your self. The following methods are suggestions. There are many variations and the reader is encouraged to use intuition and common sense. What is important to remember is that the entity is learning a lesson as well as the person hosting this spirit. It requires sending the spirit to the light, with love and some guidance. Higher protection needs to be invoked, for all involved, in the depossession. All spiritual teachers, masters, and guides of the souls present need to be invoked. The possessed soul needs to be sent to the light, out of the earth's vibrations. If not, the spirit will attach to someone else's energy system, just as in Dr. Wickland's sessions with the spirit entering his wife. We need to avoid this at all costs.

Partner Removal

After ascertaining through the chart on page 131 and your own inner knowledge, removal is more easily accomplished by having a partner working with you. Some key items to keep in mind are listed below.

- After releasing the possessing spirit, the host may experience some overt physical response such as crying, shaking, coldness or heat. The healer should be available to comfort this person. It is imperative for the individual to know what is happening.
- It is important for your partner to know that the possession was only a temporary block to his/her growth.
- The healer must clear up any negative attitudes the host has towards the entity. This can be a very traumatizing experience.
- The healer also needs to advise the person how to prevent further aura intrusions and to explain how the possession may have happened.
- The healer must be accessible to answer any questions that person may have.

When it was discovered that I was possessed, I panicked. My first response was, "What had I done to attract them?"

I felt dirty, physically and spiritually. The person who removed them needed to talk more to me and explain in greater depth the whys and wherefores. I had many questions and concerns following that experience. My greatest fear was attracting new entities. At the time, I was traumatized; now, it seems insignificant, because I can control external energies.

The following technique is written from the healer's point of view. You will be working with the higher Ascension energies of love, peace and harmony where no low or evil spirit would be comfortable. The concept behind this type of removal is to rise above the astral level of the entity. You need to contact your highest and most powerful spirit teachers and guides as well as the angelic realms.

Also, the host and entity's teachers and guides need to be available to facilitate an easy, painless transition for all. If there is any doubt or fear in your mind, have a professional remove it.

You will need a dimly lit room that has been cleansed with White Light. Candles and incense may be burned. It is helpful to have soft, tranquil music playing in the background. Make sure there will be no interruptions for the next 15 minutes or so. Have a blanket handy in case your partner gets cold and a window slightly open.

STEP ONE
- Protect yourself with the Violet Vortex, White Light and any other methods you use for protection i.e. symbols, prayers etc.
- Call in the spiritual teachers and guides that are to work with you on removals.
- Call in the entity's and partner's spirit guides and teachers.
- Call in a deceased loved one from the entity's side to help in taking it to the light.

STEP TWO
- Have your partner lie, face up on a healing table, massage table or comfortable surface so you can readily stand over and beside this person. Ensure all jewelry is removed from both of you. Nothing should obstruct the healer's movement over the body.

STEP THREE
- Put your hands on your partner's toes. Visualize removing any negativity with your hands.
- Keeping your hands directly on his/her body, slowly move them up over the ankles, calves, shins, knees and thighs. You are looking for any resistance to your pulling motion. The ankles and knees are great spots for posses-

sions to attach because, symbolically, these are the areas of the body that move us forward and they want to hold us back. You may sense a stickiness or heaviness in these areas. Keep pulling and moving up the body.

STEP FOUR
- Without removing your hands from the body, move over the genital area up to the breasts. These two spots are easy prey for possessing entities. This is where we hold judgments against others or ourselves. Both areas are outward expressions of our sexuality.

STEP FIVE
- Without lifting the hands, keep pulling over the chest and neck.
- Stop at the throat. Hold your hands on this area.
- Mentally ask any loved ones of the possessing soul to move in closer.
- Say, "I am going to count to three. When I reach three, I am going to release you to the light and your loved ones. Come and go towards the light."

STEP SIX
- Continue your pulling action over the face until you reach the top of the head.
- Mentally visualize that you are pulling all the negativity out his/her body and releasing it through the crown. The crown is where the entity will be released.
- Call in your Master Guides and those of your partner's and request the energy be taken far away from the third dimension and that this soul be healed and retrained in the higher levels.

STEP SEVEN
- Return to your partner's feet.
- Again put your hands on his/her toes and imagine she is being filled with White Light.

STEP EIGHT
- Begin the process of moving up from the feet to the head, but this time you are inserting a blazing white light, to fill his/her body, while it fortifies the aura.
- Mentally thank the higher energies for assisting you in this process.

STEP NINE
- If you wish, you may balance your partner's chakras, perform Reiki, therapeutic touch, or whatever method you use for total healing. When you are finished, cover your partner with a blanket.
- Fill your being with the Violet Vortex to ensure that you have not inadvertently picked up any residue.

STEP TEN
- Hug and comfort your partner.

Self-Depossession Technique

You need a quiet room, where there will be no disturbances, for the next twenty minutes. You may sit or lie down. Harmonizing music can be softly played. A candle or incense may be lighted to enhance positive vibrations. Be sure to have a window or door open just a crack to release the entity from your home.

STEP ONE
- Invoke a White Light around your body.

STEP TWO
- Call on any spirit guides or masters who work with you to come in and assist. Even if you consciously do not see or sense their presence, be assured they will be there. Just ask for the "highest and the best" to come and work with you. Ask to have a shield of protection around you.

STEP THREE
- Speak aloud to the invading energy.
- Tell it you are aware of its presence.
- Explain that by being caught in the third dimension there are so many pleasures and growth potentials it is missing. Explain how it missed the light when dying. Apologize if you have inadvertently kept it bound to you.
- Talk about the Spirit Hierarchy and how in order for this entity's soul to advance, release is needed from this present bondage.

STEP FOUR
- Explain how you are now calling in its teachers and guides. Perhaps a deceased loved one will also arrive, to help this soul make its transition.

STEP FIVE
- Visualize the entity being released through your crown chakra. Tell your spirit guides and masters to take this energy out of the earth's energies. Request that it be healed and retrained in the higher planes. Even if you do not see its exit, you will sense a lightness and coolness around your body.

STEP SIX
- Fill your entire being with the Violet Vortex.

STEP SEVEN
- Thank your teachers and guides for their assistance and protection.
- Thank the entity's spiritual helpers as well.
- Return to full consciousness. You may wish to do the meditation for cleansing and strengthening your aura, given at the end of this book.

If there is more than one entity, the above may need to be repeated for the removal of each.

SECTION THREE

The final section deals with the removal of ghosts and poltergeist.

GHOST BUSTING

Most ghosts are lost souls, wandering aimlessly about. They need to be directed to the light and then on to higher areas of learning. Ghosts are usually attached to a place, rather than a specific person. Some are here to guide living souls as in the case of Jake, the father of Lois. He has a karmic obligation to stick by his daughter and watch over the house. Circumstances usually do not permit this type of spirit to be discerned. Gentle ones go about their business without any manifestations.

Spirits can be gotten rid of by various methods. In Chapter 6, "The Intruders," the story about Athendorus was told. He exorcised his ghost by digging up its bones. Once this occurred, the spirit was able to move on, leaving Athendorus's house in peace.

But, generally ghost busting is not so easy. As mentioned earlier, most ghosts do not realize they no longer have a physical body with its accompanying needs. Through conversations with mediums and psychics, the missing links of information as to why a spirit is earthbound are revealed. Once the reason for it being stuck in the third dimension is understood, it usually moves towards the light.

Dr. Hazel Dennings, in *True Hauntings: Spirits with a Purpose*, cites several cases where her co-worker, a medium, convinced ghosts to stop haunting houses and retreat to the higher planes. One particular haunting in which Dennings was involved was with a woman who was being terrorized in her home. This woman felt "an eerie sensation of not being alone. She tried to raise her head to look around; to her horror, she was unable to move." This pattern repeated itself for a couple of weeks just as she was falling asleep. Finally the entity spoke to her. The woman was so afraid that she contacted Dennings and her assistant, Gertrude. Gertrude called in a discarnate friend of the ghost who convinced him to leave the earth plane. The reason the ghost gave for haunting the house was because the woman's latent psychic abilities were like a beacon attracting this lost soul.

Ghosts can recharge from the electromagnetic fields around water and mineral inclusions in rock. Water is symbolically associated with fluidity and sensitivity. It is like a tape recorder, playing back released emotions. And, because of its magnifying and attracting qualities, ghosts are drawn to places on water. Also being on or close to a quiet peaceful lake or hearing the ocean's surf caress a beach dissolves our emotional and spiritual limitations while invigorating our physical self. Whenever I am standing by a peaceful, calm, body of fresh water, my suppressed emotions drain away. I experience a longing to return to a less complicated lifestyle and am inspired creatively. I truly appreciate and hold deep within my soul the times that I am allowed to be in such an environment, one with Nature.

One "tape recorded" ghost story took place on the Georgian Bay in northern Ontario, where there is plenty of water and rock for charging spirits. My sister and her family annually rented an old cottage on its shores. The first night visiting this cottage, I was bothered by noises and scratching. Since we were in the wilds, I assumed animals were making these sounds, but the next night, I felt an eerie presence in my room and had reoccurring dreams of a young girl, trapped in the cottage.

Recounting my story the next morning, my sister confirmed that she too always felt someone watching her and also heard noises at night. I left that day and nothing more was said about it.

The following summer, the same patterns of noise and dreams were repeated when I visited. One night I "saw" the ghost. I was awakened from a deep sleep with a pressing feeling on my chest and I felt the bed clothes being moved. I then saw a ghostly image of a young girl in her nightdress, floating above me, over the bed. I sensed she had drowned at least fifty years ago and was earthbound in this building. I did not feel that she was trying to harm me, but just wanted my attention. I released her to the light by calling in her spirit guides and long-deceased parents. The room filled with a misty gray light. I heard no voices but the apparition seemed to vanish. We never encountered spirits in the cottage again.

Ghost Removal

If a ghost is sensed, the process to send it to the light is:

1. Speak directly to the entity, whether you can see it or not. Act as if the two of you were engaged in a two-way

conversation. This process must be done earnestly and sincerely. You have to assume the responsibility of helping this soul.

2. Explain to the ghost that it is dead. Try and discover how or why it died.
3. Tell it, there is no hell or place of eternal damnation. Project the thoughts of light and love waiting to embrace and relieve its bondage. Explain that it will, once again, have a strong healthy body.
4. Tell the ghost it is time to leave. Explain that the white light will arrive to protect and guide it on its journey to paradise. Promise you will say a prayer to help the ghost release itself from this dimension.
5. Call on this soul's teachers, guides and any deceased relatives.
6. See it being released and vanishing from this dimension.
7. Cleanse yourself with the Violet Vortex.
8. You may wish to further purify the room or house with incense, candles, crystals, music etc.

Remember that it does not matter whether you can see or hear it. You intuitively know an unwanted spirit is there or you would not have noticed its presence.

The following is an account of a more difficult ghost busting. Since I am unable to converse with spirits, I had to rely on my intuition and special manner of sensing energies. (The names have been changed to protect the privacy of the family).

Neighbors of mine moved their place of residence. The house they bought was approximately ten years of age and had three previous owners, all of which had interesting backgrounds.

The first owners had a teenage son who was emotionally disturbed. He hung a dummy in the basement, with artificial blood dripping out of holes he had made with a knife. I do not know if he was unbalanced before moving into the house, but the house heightened any of these latent tendencies.

The next owner had several boarders. One, an unemployed woman, sprayed her room with Holy Water each night to ward off Satan. She claimed to be following the rituals given in Ephesians 6:12 of donning her armor to protect against evil. If she neglected to do so, she felt an energy caressing her during the night. Apparently she took advantage of her landlord's generosity and was asked to leave. I am certain she must have feared something in the house and, being asked to leave, would have generated a deal of negative thought forms to add to the negative energy already present in the house. I have no follow up on the other tenant.

The next owners kept to themselves. The woman had a miscarriage. Marriage conflicts escalated to the point of separation. The house was sold to my friend and her family.

One can only assume that many incompatible energies and thought forms had permeated the house before my friends moved in.

My friend confided to me that the house felt strange. She, along with her two children and husband, would often hear footsteps and unexplained noises during the day and night. She frequently heard the outside door of the garage open and close while alone in the house. Her health was failing and the children were acting unruly, difficult to discipline. Since she knew of my interest in the spiritual world, she asked me to come over, and give my ideas as to what might be going on. In the meantime, my friend asked her neighbors for information on the previous owners.

I had been in the house a few times, before learning about these phenomena. I had uncomfortable feelings but attributed these to other things. This time, I protected myself with white light, my special symbol, a prayer for protection, an aura enhancer and crystals. When I entered the house, I sensed nothing out of the ordinary. I went to the basement where I was overcome by a heavy energy in one corner near the house's main electrical panel. I doused with my crystal pendulum to see if there was a negative energy and received an affirmation. I ignited a stick of cedar incense and opened a window. Holding a smoky quartz crystal point up in my right hand, I imagined the energy going to the light. My friend had Holy Water blessed by a pastor and I used it to make the sign of the cross over all outlets and doors. As I continued checking the basement, I felt a slight heaviness in the playroom (where the dummy had been). I again burned incense. This time, I used the violet vortex technique. The incense formed in odd shapes as it burned, and I felt that this room was the entity's home base.

My friend joined me for the rest of the house inspection. A hair-raising energy passed through both of us in the living room. The entity had moved directly above where I thought I had released it from the basement. Only this time, it was stronger and there was a strange sulfur-like odor. My friend started saying prayers while I concentrated on sending it to the light and using the Holy Water. We then burned incense and sprinkled sea salt around the room. We checked the room and felt only a small residue of negativity. Since a trail can be left behind from the spirit's energy, we were not too concerned. I left with an uneasy feeling. I asked my friend to check the living room for the next few days and report back to me. That night, I dreamed the ghost was still there. The next morning I called Jody Maas, an Energy Consultant, or ghost buster, as I teasingly called him. Jody agreed to come and test the house for possible energy intrusions. He said the entity sounded like a playful one.

Another way to test for spirits and poltergeists is dowsing. The earliest recorded dowsers were the Celts who located metals under the soil by this method. This ancient divination art originally entailed a forked stick, which was used to locate underground water. The stick was held in both hands with the vortex either upright or horizontal as the person walked over the ground. When water was located, the stick would twitch or sometimes forcibly turn downwards. Modern dowsers use rods to locate lost objects, ascertain positive and negative energies and discover weak spots in auras. What is relevant, to new age remedies for old age problems, is that an adept dowser can detect ghosts, thought forms and poltergeists.

Jody is a skilled dowser who identifies "noxious water" veins under homes using metal rods. He started dowsing around my friend's home. At each spot where the rods swung to the left, Jody sprinkled a spoonful of a special combination of dried incense on the ground. He explained to us that he was dowsing for noxious veins of water that directly effect the energies surrounding the people living in the house. The veins were not evil in themselves but they were attraction points for low-life spirits and energies. The greatest number he had ever encountered at one house was fourteen. This house had thirty-four.

When he had completed sprinkling all negative entry spots outside, Jody went into the basement. He, too, was drawn to the electrical panel area. As well as water, ghosts are attracted to the raw energy of electricity. Jody spent a great deal of time cleansing the playroom area, burning incense and clearing with white light. He too sensed this was one of the entity's locations.

He then sprinkled his special mixture of equal parts of sand, sulfur and salt on all electrical outlets, drains and toilets. All possible entrances for the noxious veins were christened. His final depossession technique was to burn his incense in each room, to clear all possible residue of negativity.

While we were back in the basement lighting incense, Jody was drawn to a wall, near the electrical panel with two metal spears nailed to it. The spears' tips were pointing into the back of a woodcarving that resembled the figure of a man. We both sensed a great deal of heavy energy in this area.

My skin prickled, my breathing became rapid and I felt as if someone were strangling me. Jody quickly released this energy from the spears and from me by sending it to the light. My friend's invading ghost was gone!

The house was very volatile, due to the underground water problems and the type of people who had been attracted to living in this house. We never heard the spirit speak or knew why it was earthbound. Perhaps it was there before the house was built. As far as I can ascertain, the house had both an entity and negative thought forms. If the energies had not been removed, poltergeist activity would most likely have occurred.

Many factors need be taken into consideration when releasing ghosts or poltergeists. The house itself may be the attracting force rather than the people living in it. But the people will be somehow affected. There is always a common theme between the entity and the people. It plays on their weaknesses, making them escalate, as with the teenager hanging up the dummy, the unemployed boarder, the marriage breakup and my friend's ill health.

POLTERGEIST REMOVAL

Poltergeists are removed in much the same way as ghosts. The young person alluded to in the *Exorcist* (the true story was a boy, not a girl) had his poltergeist removed by several priests and members of the Church, performing a series of rituals over a number of days using chants, prayers and incense.

A similar situation occurred in Pontefract, England, when a house made headlines with its poltergeist activities. The haunting included doors slamming, ceiling paint falling, flooding, distinctive odors, beds shaking, furniture moving, electricity and electrical appliance failures. The family was experiencing some difficult emotional problems, as well. A psychic discovered the family's 13- and 15-year-olds were energizing the poltergeist. Whenever they complained of stomach problems, the strange occurrences would start. Poltergeists were drawing on the children's solar plexus for power to manifest destructive behavior. Holy water and garlic were used to stop the haunting. What makes this story of particular interest is the house was built on the location where once was a bridge over a (now dried up) stream. It was also near an old gallows. The house most certainly had noxious water veins. It was further influenced by all the dead souls and negative thought forms around the gallows as well as the emotional states of the inhabitants of the house (Wilson, 1981, pp. 137–71).

To exorcise poltergeists, we can rely on the wisdom of our forefathers. If at all possible, it is advisable to enlist the help of an experienced ghost buster. But, it can be done on our own by following these steps and our own intuitiveness.

1. Fortify your aura by whatever method works best for you.
2. Decide on whether to use Holy Water, incense, salt, crystals or candles or all five to release the destructive energies.

   Holy Water can be obtained from a place of worship or made by you. Just hold distilled or regular water in a glass container and send energy into it through prayer or visualizing white light pouring into every molecule of the water. It is the thought projections and the belief in its powers that charges the water.

3. Dowse, using rods or a pendulum, around the exterior of the house to locate the noxious water veins.
4. Sprinkle dried incense or Jody's salt mixture over these spots (2 or 3 tablespoons should be sufficient).
5. Inside the house, dowse for possible energy disturbances.
6. Block off all electrical outlets and openings to the outside with Holy Water or by sprinkling the salt mixture over them.
7. Clear each room with a white light and follow up with incense burning. Remember to open windows.

FURTHER SUGGESTIONS

As we have been discovering, the most important "cure" for negative energies is altering our thinking patterns from a negative to a positive nature. We need to fill ourselves from within with loving, accepting energies. Remember, like attracts like, and as St. Paul said so adeptly in Galatians 6:7, "Whatsoever a man soweth, that shall he also reap."

Nothing negative can affect us unless we are open to it. If a partner is angry or swears at us, remember that this person is really mad at her/himself. It is our choice whether we want to take on his "stuff" and suffer along with him/her. Misery loves company!

Our mission, in this new millennium, is to strengthen our auras. Our energies need to be shielded against the entry of undesirable forces that surround us. Right this minute, you, the reader, have the conscious choice of taking charge of your life or leaving it up to the energies around you. Only you can facilitate the change.

We no longer need to be the victim.

We are the VICTORS!

INVADING ENERGY CHART

REMEDIES	INVADING ENERGIES						
CURES	THOUGHT FORMS	POSSESSIONS	PLACES	PEOPLE	ASTRAL DEBRIS	GHOSTS	POLTERGEIST
Affirmations	X						
Aura Devices	X	X	X	X	X		
Body Crossing			X	X	X		
Candles	X	X	X	X	X	X	X
Crystals	X	X	X	X	X	X	X
Essences	X						
Flower Remedies	X	X				X	X
Gem Elixirs	X	X				X	X
Hand Claps	X	X	X	X	X	X	
Incense	X	X	X	X	X	X	X
Love Energy	X	X	X	X	X	X	X
Music	X	X	X	X	X	X	X
Parasite Technique					X		
Possession Removal		X					
Psychic Attack Remov.	X			X			
Prayer	X	X	X	X	X	X	X
Salt Mixture		X	X	X	X	X	X
Wall				X			
Water			X	X	X		
White Light	X	X	X	X	X	X	X
Violet Vortex	X	X	X	X	X	X	X
Symbol	X	X	X	X	X	X	X

CHAPTER EIGHT

Shedding Light on Darkness

ALL IN THE WORLD of entities and thought forms is not darkness. Much light, wonderment, joy and benediction comes when we are in touch with spirit guides and teachers. Connections are made with Universal Consciousness. New truths and insights can be revealed. Higher input is received for daily life activities. Past-life information becomes accessible. Existing blockages are overcome. Spiritual growth is stimulated, bringing us closer to a complete union with soul. Our consciousness and that of this planet is elevated.

It is not difficult to determine the difference between a dark and light entity. With the latter, a deep sense of peace and loving resonance is present. The feeling is similar stepping into a warm, soothing bath. Helpful and highly evolved spirits never permanently possess a human's body or mind without permission. They are here to assist and guide. A bone-chilling sensation, shrouded with fear and heaviness, like the cold treacherous waters of a raging sea, identifies the presence of a lower entity. Dark entities overtake without consent and use us to fulfill their own needs.

Yet, encounters with lower energies should not be viewed as something dark and sinister. Although their presence around us can be frightening, it is truly an opportunity for self-growth and development. If I had not had my possessing entities and unsolicited experience with the spirit world, I would not have arrived at my current state of comfort and peace with all thought and spirit forms.

Trials and tribulations advance us to our next stage of spiritual development. We both subconsciously and consciously choose our experiences so vital lessons can be learned. We never make "mistakes," just attract opportunities for growth. The trauma of seeing a **ghost**, having a **possession,** being the recipient of a **psychic** or **human parasite** attack, influenced by **astral garbage** or **negative thought** forms, may be just the necessary incentive to push us forward.

The benefits of being in touch with spiritual teachers, masters, angels and guides are numerous. Once our auras are protected and thoughts clearer, our physical and spiritual well-being is enhanced by direct contact with these highly evolved beings. The positive aspects of being in touch with the higher energies are:

1) When feeling the onset of flu, cold or other virus, the ability to call on spirit teachers for healing and help to discover why you have opened yourself to illness can lessen the length and intensity of the sickness.

2) If you have a serious illness, asking the masters and meditating as to what this infliction is teaching you or others around you will help give you inner strength and fortitude. Calling on the healing angels helps eliminate some of the physical discomfort. You may be guided to a new type of treatment or ways to lessen your attitude towards the illness.

3) You can contact and channel the highest and best energies for healing others. When I am doing massage or

crystal healing work on others, I often feel a pair of ancient, experienced, healing hands taking charge of my own. More information flows as to how to help determine my partner's real needs.

4) Call on spiritual help to soothe children who are emotionally or physically hurt. As parents, you have spiritual permission to assist your child in the highest way possible. Call in their guides and those of your own to facilitate healing.

As a young child, when my son was physically hurt from bumping into things or falling off his bike, he would instantly create a web of revenge and hatred towards us. He always said his Dad or I had hurt him. In his mind, we were directly responsible for this injury, even if we were not present. I learned to counteract his outbreaks by enclosing him with the Violet Vortex and asking his spirit guides to dissipate the negative energies and quickly heal his physical and emotional wounds.

5) Fewer transgressions are committed in physical, earthly matters because you rely not only on your intuition but receive guidance from higher forces as well.

6) Relationships improve. Being more aware of the many forces and influences of unseen energies affecting people makes you a more empathetic person. If a child or partner acts in an uncharacteristic way, your reaction will be one of understanding and support. Calling on your teachers and guides will help you see the situation in a totally different way.

7) Daily life is easier to cope with because its challenges are understood and accepted. Just knowing higher guidance is available is a comfort.

8) You are more protected against all types of negativity from people, places, entities and thought forms.

9) Fear is removed towards unseen forces.

10) Universal Consciousness is available for you to use in your life's work. Creativity, happiness, unconditional love and prosperity are all there waiting to embrace you.

11) You are able to find your own answers and truths to perplexing questions such as, "Why have I chosen to incarnate at this time?" "What lesson am I to learn from this person?" "Why did I attract this entity into my aura?" and so on. You have your own direct pipeline to higher truths. Often, people seek out psychics or readers to solve their problems, when the answers are right before them.

12) Past lives are revealed through contact with spirit guides.

13) Any form of spirit communication, such as automatic writing or tarot readings, is heightened and enhanced. Having a well-developed third-eye center was discussed in "The Veil Is Lifted," Chapter 4. Although a novice needs to proceed with care, there are many experienced, protected readers, writers and divination people who reap enormous benefits, personally and professionally, from their connection with higher forces.

14) A final joy, of connecting with the higher spiritual realms, is channeling.

Channeling is a further step towards spiritual awakening. It is a natural progression, establishing a conscious link with soul and the higher energies. Channelers are the people who communicate with thoughts and energies of higher spiritual beings in the angelic, master and upper levels. The entities do not usually predict the future, as psychics do, nor permit a conversation with deceased relatives. These entities are more interested in imparting knowledge and guidance as to how humankind can incorporate the higher spiritual ideals into their lives.

Channeling can be done in a **deep trance** or **conscious state**. **Trance** occurs when the channeler is in a completely altered state of being. This person has no conscious recollection of what is being said. S/he appears to have temporarily stepped out of his/her body. The voice may be pitched deeper or higher than normal. The words may be pronounced slower. There may be an accent; dialect alteration or antiquated language may be used. Body and facial alterations occur. Mannerisms are different from those of the host. Trance workers give **conscious permission** for an entity or group of entities to use their body for the transmission of information.

Edgar Cayce was one of the most notable trance channelers in the 20th century. He transmitted ancient healing techniques, prophesied the future, and revealed information about lost civilizations. J.Z. Knight channeled an entity named Ramtha, who was from the lost continent of Lemuria. In the 1980s J.Z. had a large following who implemented her entity's teachings in their daily lives. Kevin Ryerson, who achieved world recognition through Shirley MacLaine's *Out on a Limb,* channeled the Apostle Paul.

Bart Smit, a deep trance channeler residing in Toronto, Ontario, channels an entity by the name of Dr. Williams. Bart appears on numerous radio and television shows and travels worldwide, spreading the spiritual teachings of Dr. Williams. To enlighten us as to how a deep trance channeler and a discarnate work together, Bart shared the following information.

Bart was born in Holland. As an infant, he had strange markings on one of his thighs like scars from stitches. An inner ear problem and dyslexia afforded him the unique experience of attending a special private school, where meditation and right-brain thinking were part of the curriculum. Bart learned how to feel and approach life from a global perspective.

His first contact with the astral plane took place as a young child. He knew things about other people and would blurt them out. His accurate perception embarrassed his family and he was told to be quiet. Suppressing this natural spiritual spontaneity resulted in Bart feeling out of control and alone. He thought everyone had these same perceptions and could not understand why he was being disciplined. It was only when time was spent horseback riding in natural settings, that he felt peace and control in his abilities.

Around the age of 13 Bart sensed an unseen force around him, but he had no fear of this energy because it surrounded him with loving acceptance.

At 26, Bart came to terms with his spirituality. He attended his first channeling session and knew with absolute certainty this was how he was to communicate and teach others. He just needed to bring his destiny into focus.

A friend helped Bart develop conscious awareness of this ever-present energy around him. During meditation, he would fall into a deep, deep, state of relaxation. He heard voices: a man, with a British accent. His entire body expanded to accommodate a larger presence. Dr. Roy Williams had come through! This entity spoke about planetary changes, human behavior, universal laws, truths and wisdom beyond any knowledge Bart had ever been exposed to.

The two of them kindled a deep karmic tie that started many lifetimes ago. Williams' last lifetime was in South Africa. An archeologist from Oxford had gone to this country, met Williams, and brought him back to England as a household slave. As he did not have a last name, Roy took the family name of his master, Williams. The title of Dr. is from two previous lifetimes, when he was a Professor of Psychology and Philosophy at Oxford University.

In 1846, Williams returned to Africa, reuniting with his brother (Bart in this lifetime). Williams found him very ill with an infection from a leg injury spreading throughout his body. This is when Dr. Williams amputated his brother's leg, saving his life. The marks Bart was born with were further proof of a sign from spirit. When Bart was told the reason for the markings, they began to mysteriously fade.

Bart explained that the first few years of channeling Dr. Williams, he had some discomfort assimilating the larger man's energies. Now, only his mannerisms and speech differ, indicating it is Williams, and not Bart, who is present.

Bart is not consciously aware of what transpires during a client session. He made this agreement with Dr. Williams in order to not get involved with these people's lives and problems. Bart's clients consult this higher spirit to ascertain answers to queries about spiritual growth, karmic ties, relationships, dreams, spiritual guides, and teachers and careers. He also gets referrals from psychiatrists whose clients have blocked out childhood memories and have multiple personalities.

Bart made a conscious choice to work with spirit. As well, it is his decision to be a deep trance channeler so he can fully let others experience the energies and wisdom of his entity.

There is also **conscious channeling,** which each of us performs, in one way or another. No two persons will channel energies in the same manner. Some channel verbally, others in written form, when healing, helping others or while performing routine tasks. Inspiration can manifest as if from nowhere, encouraging us to start or complete a project.

I had much help from spirit writing this book. I was directed to many people, places and books that inspired and encouraged me. As mentioned at the beginning, I also had encounters with lower entities that tried to discourage me. However, I knew that light would overrule darkness and kept on with my work.

Suddenly finding the solution to a nagging problem is a form of channeling. Spirit has given or shown us the answer. Often we spout out astonishing words of wisdom that we know comes from somewhere other than ourselves because it is different from our normal thinking. A mother channels healing energies to relieve her child of a fever. Artists channel works of art in the form of paintings, books, music etc.

An aware channeler, in control of the situation, can ask and receive answers. This person's mind acts as a third party, having stepped aside from the personality and emotions, but not the body. If the channeling is in the form of ideas, then divine inspiration will prompt the artist to pick up his brush, the writer his pen, and the scientist his test tubes.

It matters not how channeling is done. It is the connection and spiritual growth that occurs when these higher beings are contacted.

To channel is to reach beyond the limitations of the mind. It links with soul, enabling you to receive direct energy from the Universal realms. You are connected with higher wisdom and overwhelming vibrations of love allowing you to be more attuned with all that is. These are only a few benefits of connecting with higher spirits and guides. The guided meditation technique, given at the end of this book, will help you to reach into these spiritual levels.

As a final note on the benefits of spirit connection, by tapping into higher forces, the possibilities for growth and spiritual advancement are limitless. Doors open to self-awareness that were previously closed. Enrichment comes into all aspects of our physical and spiritual lives. Light is shed on darkness.

TO SEE YOUR DRAMA CLEARLY
IS TO BE LIBERATED FROM IT.

Ken Keyes Jr.
Handbook to Higher Consciousness

CHAPTER NINE

We Do Not Die

EACH ONE OF US MUST DECIDE whether or not to embrace our spiritual path, while keeping in mind that it is our mission to gain as much information as possible about our spiritual selves while we are on this earth.

Those that have no belief system or refuse to acknowledge their journey are chained to third-dimensional life. They are not ready to see the world in a different light. Being unwilling to explore and listen to others' thoughts and beliefs, these living people are earthbound by their own narrow thought patterns. They lack faith to reach into the light and beyond limitations in this life. And in death, they have the possibility of remaining as **Entities Among Us.**

Everyone progresses at his or her own rate. The amount of spiritual growth achieved depends on a number of factors. Some of these are:
- **where we started from**
- **how deeply our subconscious negative thoughts are embedded**
- **what catalysts or situations are presented to force change**
- **what our soul has incarnated to accomplish and the drive of our personality, i.e., how strong our will is**

- **how much we want to change and if we accept our lessons and are able to learn from new experiences.**

When we chose to come into this life, we knew the journey would not be easy. Yet each of us has an inner spark of divinity. We are as much apart of the higher dimensions as we are of earth. Therefore, we need be careful to not harm ourselves through such detrimental actions as over indulging in lower vibrational activities like drinking, gambling, or sex that is not accompanied with love, or participating in any action that is not in our truth. And, to help us along, a new dawn has arrived with ascension energies being channeled towards this planet. These incredible forces allow us to be in touch with every dimension of light, the totality of ourselves, and to achieve harmonious synchronicity with all living matter. The choice is ours, to sit and wallow in darkness, or progress into the light.

Negative thought forms and spirit encounters are all part of the trials and tribulations along the path of spiritual growth. The Biblical verse, Romans 8:37, states that, "Through trials we are more than conquerors because our consciousness profits from every experience." Inner strength, faith and fortitude are achieved in the end.

There are four steps to overcoming the trials of unwanted energy intrusions. We must first become aware of the type and source of the invasion; next, we need to determine why the energy was attracted to our aura; thirdly, the unwanted entity or attack needs to be banished; and lastly, we need to protect our aura from further intrusions.

If there were no strife in our lives, we would fail to grow and learn. Stagnation would set in. There would be no reason to move ahead or alter our thinking processes. Therefore, we must take the chance and embrace the unlimited benefits available on this journey.

A few of these are:

- We see things from a broader perspective
- We allow others to express their inner selves without criticism or judgment
- We accept our lessons and take responsibility for our actions
- We no longer need people and circumstances in our lives that victimize or attack us
- We accept that every experience is chosen by the higher self
- We can manifest the requirements for fun and joy in our lives
- The higher your level of consciousness, the more rapidly inner peace is restored following an upset.

Our spiritual development is an adventure into uncharted regions. We undergo a transformation, a raising of consciousness into higher and higher levels. We are in the process of preparing ourselves to fully embrace the Ascension energies. Wonderment, excitement, beauty and joy override any possible dangers.

We have purpose in our lives. This lifetime is but a temporary stopover, where we learn as much as possible, in order to graduate to the next level. Transition awaits each and every one of us, but ... **WE DO NOT DIE.**

APPENDIX

HARMONIZING AURA PROTECTION
MEDITATION

The following meditation is a chakra balance and visualization to protect the aura. This meditation transcript can be taped with soft music playing in the background.

STEP ONE
- Create a quiet serene environment. Ensure you will not be disturbed for the next 20 minutes. Lie comfortably on your back, arms at your sides.

STEP TWO
- Take a deep breath. Hold it for the count of 3. Release for 3.
- Take another deep breath. Hold for 3. And exhale for 3.
- Take another breath. As you exhale, allow the last remnants of tension to flow away.

STEP THREE
- Now count backwards from 9 to 1.
  9, your breathing is deep and regular
  8, you are going deeper and deeper into a meditative state
  7, your body, mind and spirit are at rest
  6, deeper and deeper into relaxation
  5, you are feeling more relaxed and at peace then you have ever felt before

4, you are going deeper and deeper into a place of inner stillness

3, you are feeling more and more at peace

2, you are descending further and further

1, you are now drifting and floating in a complete state of relaxation.

STEP FOUR

Imagine the outer limits of your aura being extended 6 feet in all directions. Now extend your personal energy field 6 feet from your head, 6 feet from your feet, 6 feet from your back and 6 feet from your front. You have now created an elliptical cocoon of energy all around your body. Float in the center of its comforting vibrations.

STEP FIVE

Now focus your attention on your base chakra. Feel a gentle warmth and pressure over this area.

Picture a beautiful, closed red lotus flower, one the dawn has not yet reached with her soft golden rays of warmth. Allow these flower petals to open slowly in a ritualistic dance, one by one. You are now able to go forward with your life. When the petals are all opened to the light, mentally project this vibrant red color at your base chakra. See the red as a beam of light. Direct it higher and higher, at least 6 feet, to the inner ceiling of your aura. Now imagine this brilliant hue encompassing your entire aura, filling it with red. And it is done.

Focus your attention over the spleen center. See a closed orange lotus bud over this area.

Imagine now, the gentle golden rays of the sun unfolding each delicate petal in slow motion. Feel the freedom when the flower is fully opened. Now, you can fully accept who you are—without judgment. Mentally project that orange vibrant color at your spleen chakra into a beam of light. Project it higher and higher, at least 6 feet, out to the inner ceiling of your aura. Imagine this brilliant hue encompassing your entire aura, filling it with orange. And it is done.

Now imagine a closed, yellow-hued lotus resting softly over your solar plexus. Open each fragile petal to the warmth of the sun. See it happening slowly and naturally as the warmth reaches into your very center. You are taking back your power. Mentally project this yellow color at your solar plexus into a beam of light going higher and higher, at least 6 feet, filling your entire aura. Imagine this brilliant hue encompassing your entire aura, filling it up with yellow. And it is done.

Move up now to the tiny pink bud lying over your heart center, in the middle of your chest. Gently open and release the powerful healing energies of each petal. As the flower opens, so does your unconditional love for yourself and all of God's creation. Push that illuminating pink shade out of this center until it completely fills your aura. Remember you will always have that pink hue of love inside your being. And, it is done.

Focus your attention now over the azure blue, unopened flower resting over your throat, your area of expression. The sun gently coaxes each petal, covered with the moist dew of the early dawn, into opening to the light. Now, mentally project this azure color at your throat up higher and higher, at least 6 feet, to the inner shell of your aura. Imagine this brilliant hue encompassing your entire aura, filling it up with blue. And it is done.

Visualize the velvet indigo, unopened flower resting over your third eye, your window to your inner self and other dimensions. As you open each soft petal to the brilliant sunlight, unlock your inner self-being; unlock and open your being to the light. Feel that image as it activates your inner seeing. Mentally project this azure color at your throat, up higher and higher, at least 6 feet, to the inner shell of your aura. Imagine this brilliant hue encompassing your entire aura, filling it up with indigo. And it is done.

Now focus your attention on the violet sleeping lotus flower, resting on your crown chakra. Project the golden light of the sun down on it. Allow its virgin petals to open slowly in a ritualistic dance, one by one. When all the petals are opened to the light, this center will be fully energized. Feel yourself energize, as your connection with the Universe, and all that is, has been once again reestablished. Pump this violet light to the insides of your aura. And it is done.

STEP SIX

Now mentally image a White Light directly on your base chakra. You are going to push that light up from your base into all the centers.

Let us begin.

See it travelling up the center of your body from the base to the spleen, the spleen to the solar plexus, the solar plexus to the heart, the heart to the throat, the throat to the third eye and the third eye to the crown. Your inner circuit is complete.

Now visualize your entire aura pulsating with white light. Your body and aura are full of the brilliance of this light.

STEP SEVEN

Now that your 7 main centers are activated and your aura's colors energized, you are ready to fully protect the aura.

Visualize that you are, once again, floating in the center of a cocoon shape. Surrounding your physical body are layers containing your etheric, emotional and mental bodies. See these layers as moving elliptical energies. The shell of the aura encompasses these layers. Being inside, you can see through the outer shell out into the astral plane. See the shell as one completely unbroken line of continuous light vibrating in a brilliant golden tone. No negative energy can permeate through this protective shell. Only light and higher energies will be allowed to filter through. If you have a special symbol of protection (see Chapter 6, New Age Remedies for Old Age Problems) project that image now into all parts of your aura. You are now impervious to all negative intrusion. You are protected.

STEP EIGHT
   Float in this suspended state of relaxation.
   Look outside into the astral plane and the dimensions beyond.
   Wait and see what images, sensations or sounds come to you.

STEP NINE
   When you are ready, count yourself back to full consciousness from 1 to 9.

MEDITATION TWO
MEETING YOUR SPIRIT MASTER

   This meditation will connect you with a Master teacher. Each time you meet with your Master, greater and higher truths will be revealed. An expansion of consciousness will take place.

STEP ONE
   Sit or lie where you will not be disturbed for the next 20 minutes.
   Count yourself down to a deep state of relaxation by using the induction technique given in the previous meditation.

STEP TWO

Your mind is becoming quieter and quieter.

You are at peace.

You have moved beyond all distractions. Your mind is shifting from the world of solids and hard shapes.

You are going on a journey to meet your special spiritual Master. The angels have created a special spot for your connection to this special Being of Light.

STEP THREE

You are now standing at the end of a dock, in dawn's early mists. You can hear the gentle lapping of the waves beneath your feet. You look down and see a small gondola. This is the boat that will take you across the calm, peaceful water to a special island where you will meet your Master.

Step down into the boat. Settle in for your journey. No need to take the oars, for the angels will power it across the water. As the gondola picks up speed, you feel the gentle breeze in your hair and you begin to think what your Master will be like. You have already sensed this Being's presence but have not been consciously aware of it.

The early morning mist begins to lift and you see in the distance an island appearing.

The mist has completely cleared and you are now approaching this island.

You step off the boat, onto the conveniently positioned dock.

In the distance, you see a path that leads to a stone, pyramid-shaped structure. As you walk along this well-traveled pathway, the sight of the tall, magnificent pine trees lining the way awes you. You can actually hear the tingling harmony of the pine cones as they gently sway in the soft breezes. You energize yourself by taking in a deep breath, breathing in the prana, the life force of the green pine needles.

Right ahead, in front of the entrance to this special temple is a waterfall, one like you have never seen before. It is a cascade of all the colors of the rainbow. It will cleanse away any of the denser energies you have accumulated in your aura. Step into it now. Feel the lazy, liquid water falling on your head, face, shoulders, chest, arms, legs and feet. Be aware of the vibrant colors of pink, green, blue, yellow, orange, red and violet as all negativity washes away from your being. Any fear, doubt, anxiety, anger, hatred, jealously, unworthiness and all the energies you no longer need are now being dissolved.

You are now ready to enter the ancient pyramid temple beyond the waterfall. The doorway is open, beckoning you.

You enter the temple. There is only one room, an exact replica of the King's Chamber in the Great Pyramid of Giza. You sit on one of the two soft, comfortable cushions awaiting you on the stone floor, in the center of this temple. You look up to the apex. It is not closed but open to the sunlight. Tiny beams of light are dancing around you. You sense an expanse of energy in the room. Your entirety is flooded with joy as a shining Being of Light enters the same doorway you did. Your Master comes and sits in front of you on the other cushion. You see this person as a woman, man or an androgynous being. It is up to you to experience the Master in any form or shape that is right for you. This highly evolved Master is smiling at you, beaming warm acceptance. Your very being resonates with a feeling of coming home to the light. Your inner vision and hearing are expanding. You are overcoming any doubts you may have had about meeting such a spiritual teacher.

STEP FOUR

Converse with your Master.

Ask what the Master has to say to you.

Seek unconditional love, wisdom and higher ideals.

Know that each time you come, more and more answers will be revealed to you.

Stay as long as you like in this room, knowing that, when you return to full consciousness, peace, understanding, light and harmony will go with you into your everyday life.

Bibliography

Anderson, George. *We Don't Die*. New York: G.P. Putnam's Sons, 1985.

Bach, Edward. *The Bach Flower Remedies*. New Canaan: Keats Publishing Inc., 1979.

Bowman, Catherine. *Crystal Awareness*. Llewellyn Publications., 1987.

Bowman, Catherine. *Crystal Ascension*. Llewellyn Publications., 1996.

Budge, E.A. Wallis. *The Egyptian Book of the Dead*. New York: Dover Publications, 1967.

Cott, Jonathan. *The Search for Omm Sety*. New York: Warner Books, 1987.

Denning, Melita and Osborne Phillips. *The Truth About Psychic Self-Defence*. St. Paul: Llewellyn Publications, 1987.

Dennings, Dr. Hazel. *True Hauntings*. St. Paul: Llewellyn Publications, 1996.

Dorland, Frank. *Holy Ice*. St. Paul: Galde Press, 1992.

Eadie, Betty. *Embraced by the Light*. Placerville: Gold Leaf Press, 1992.

Fiore, Edith. *The Unquiet Dead*. New York: Ballentine Books, 1987.

Fisher, Joe. *Life Between Life*. New York: Doubleday, 1986.

Fortune, Dion. *Psychic Self Defense*. York Beach: Samuel Weiser, 1982.

Fraser, Sylvia. *The Quest for the Fourth Monkey.* Key Porter Books, 1994.

Grof, Stanislav and Christine Grof. *Spiritual Emergency.* Los Angeles: Jeremy Tarcher, 1989.

Guiley, Rosemary. *The Encyclopedia of Ghosts and Spirits.* Oxford: Roundhouse Publishing Ltd., 1992.

Gurudas. *Gem Elixirs and Vibrational Healing Volume 1.* Boulder: Cassandra Press, 1985.

Hayward, Susan. *A Guide For the Advanced Soul.* Crows Nest: In Tune Books, 1985.

Hervey, Sheila. *Canada Ghost to Ghost.* Toronto: Stoddart Books, 1998.

Hoffman, Enid. *Huna – A Beginner's Guide.* Gloucester: Para Research Inc., 1976.

Holy Bible. New York: American Bible House, 1898.

Howells, Harvey. *Dowsing Mind Over Matter.* Brattleboro: The Stephen Greene Press, 1982.

Humann, Harvey. *The Many Faces of Angels.* Marina Del Rey: DeVorss, 1986.

Randolph, Keith. *The Truth About Psychic Self-Defence.* St. Paul: Llewellyn Publications, 1987.

Reader's Digest Association Limited, The. *Strange Stories, Amazing Facts.* Montreal: Readers Digest, 1975.

Ronner, John. *Know Your Angels.* Murfreesboro: Mamre Press, 1993.

Tansley, David. *Radionics Interface with the Ether Fields.* Bradford: Health Science Press, 1975.

Time-Life Books. *The Enchanted World – Ghosts.* Alexandria: 1984.

Wickland, Carl. *Thirty Years Among the Dead.* Toronto: Coles Publishing, 1980.

Wilson, Colin. *Poltergeist.* Seven Oaks: New English Library, 1981.

Yogananda, Paramahansa. *Autobiography of a Yogi.* London: Century Hutchinson, 1950.

About the Author

Catherine Bowman's first best-seller, *Crystal Awareness* (Llewellyn Publications, 1987), has been translated into ten different languages, selling over 150,000 copies worldwide. It continues to guide thousands of people on their journey to better health, self-worth and personal power.

Her second book, *Crystal Ascension* (Llewellyn Publications, 1996), directs her readers to the next step towards self-transformation.

Ms. Bowman has appeared on TV, radio shows, book-signings, book talks and personal transformation seminars. She teaches Second Language and Learning for disabled children in the public school system, employing her degrees in Psychology and Education. She is a mother, wife, teacher, student and writer. She was born and raised in Toronto, Ontario, and has lived in the Middle East.

Ms. Bowman's interest in the paranormal began at an early age. As a young child, she sensed unseen vibrations and thought forms emanating from people, places and things. These unexplained phenomena left her feeling afraid, alone and spiritually vulnerable. It wasn't until later in life, after making the commitment to develop her own spiritual awareness, that Ms. Bowman was consciously able to discern the sources of these frightening, yet fascinating, energies.

While actively researching the subject of menacing unseen forces, **the author relieved people, houses and workplaces of undesirable vibrations.** No longer did the presence of negative energies emanating from people, places, objects, ghosts and entities conjure fear and uncertainty. Instead, she meets the challenge by first seeking the source and then eliminating adverse energies. Ms. Bowman feels that the entities among us need not control our lives. These various intrusions are here for us to remove, release to the light and learn from.

Since the completion of *Entities Among Us,* the author has written two novels in which she has woven spiritual truths into past life experiences: *Lifting the Veil* and *Daughter of the Flame.* She currently lives in southern Ontario, Canada, with her husband and teenage son.

Printed in the United States
42576LVS00002B/20